IMAGES
of Sport

WEST BROMWICH
ALBION

100 YEARS AT THE HAWTHORNS

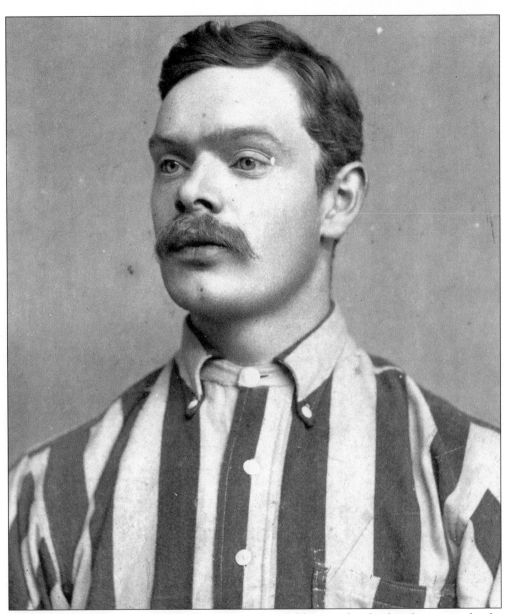

Joe Reader was Albion's goalkeeper for sixteen years and he was also the first 'keeper to play for the club in a game at The Hawthorns. Indeed, he is the only Albion player to have appeared in competitive matches on three of the club's major grounds – The Four Acres and Stoney Lane being the other two. Reader, nicknamed 'Kicker', joined Albion in January 1885 and retired as a player in April 1901. During that time he appeared in some 500 first team matches (370 at competitive level), gained an FA Cup winners' medal in 1892 and collected a runners-up prize in the same competition three years later. He won a single England cap (against Ireland in 1894) and represented the Football League on three occasions. He continued to work at The Hawthorns until 1950, first as a trainer, then trainer/coach and later as a steward. He was associated with West Bromwich Albion for a total of sixty-five years. Born in West Bromwich in 1866, Reader was the only Albion goalkeeper to be sent-off at senior level, receiving his marching orders in a League game against Bolton Wanderers in 1895. He died in March 1954 at the age of eighty-eight.

IMAGES
of Sport

WEST BROMWICH ALBION

100 YEARS AT THE HAWTHORNS

Compiled by
Tony Matthews

TEMPUS

Tempus Publishing Limited
The Mill, Brimscombe Port,
Stroud, Gloucestershire, GL5 2QG

ISBN 0 7524 2056 9

Typesetting and origination by
Tempus Publishing Limited
Printed in Great Britain by
Midway Clark Printing, Wiltshire

Also available from Tempus Publishing

Birmingham City FC	Tony Matthews	0 7524 1862 9
Bristol Rovers FC	Mike Jay	0 7524 1150 0
Exeter City FC: 1904-1994	Dave Fisher/Gerald Gosling	0 7524 1167 5
Final Tie	Norman Shiel	0 7524 1669 3
The Football Programme	John Litster	0 7524 1855 6
Forever England	Mark Shaoul/Tony Williamson	0 7524 2042 9
Leeds United FC	David Saffer	0 7524 1642 1
Northampton Town FC	John Watson/David Walden	Summer 2000
Oxford United FC	Jon Murray	0 7524 1183 7
Plymouth Argyle FC	Gordon Sparks	0 7524 1185 3
Reading FC: 1871-1997	David Downs	0 7524 1061 X
Stoke City FC	Tony Matthews	0 7524 1698 7
Swindon Town FC	Richard Mattick	Summer 2000
Torquay United FC	Mike Holgate	0 7524 1814 9
1966 World Cup	Norman Shiel	0 7524 2045 3
Bristol RFC	Mark Hoskins/Dave Fox	0 7524 1875 0
Cardiff RFC	Duncan Gardiner/Alan Evans	0 7524 1608 1
The Five Nations Story	David Hands	0 7524 1851 3

Contents

The Woodman public house still occupies the same position it did before The Hawthorns was built in 1900. In fact, the walls of the Albion ground are formed around the garden of the pub itself and nowadays it is frequented, certainly on matchdays, by avid and long-serving Baggies supporters. It could well be one of the oldest football pubs in the country.

Acknowledgements

There are so many people I would like to thank for assisting me in the compilation of this special book to commemorate the 100th anniversary of the opening of The Hawthorns. To mention them all would take an extra half page at least. However, I must say a special thank you to the following for supplying quite a few photographs and/or newspaper cuttings: Kevin Grice, Barry Marsh, Laurie Rampling, Adam Fradgley (*Sunday Mercury*, Birmingham), Glenn Willmore, Paul Leddington, Alan Cleverley, Dean Walton, Michael Reynolds, Ron Chew, Keith Simcox and Mrs Margaret Holliday – all of them avid Albion supporters!

There are a handful of ex-players, namely Ray Barlow, Wilf Carter, Glyn Hood, Jimmy Sanders and Dave Walsh, as well as former Albion physiotherapist Fred Pedley, to whom I am particularly grateful for loaning photographs from their personal collections.

I must thank three more ardent Albion supporters who, in a small way, have assisted me with information regarding the players, matches and so on: Colin Mackenzie, Robert Bradley and John Homer. I also cannot forget my loving wife Margaret, who once again has had to put up with me grunting and groaning while tip-tapping away at the keyboard – all good fun though, hey!

There are, of course, many more people – young and old or sadly no longer with us – who have done their little bit for West Bromwich Albion Football Club and worked at The Hawthorns to to make it what it was and what it is today. Without them a book such as this could not have been published.

Introduction

The Hawthorns, believed to be the highest League ground above sea level in the United Kingdom at 551 feet, has been home to West Bromwich Albion Football Club since 1900. Situated on the main A41 road leading to and from Birmingham and less than a mile from the M5/M6 motorway junction, it was called The Hawthorns because the land it was built on was shown on the surveyor's map as The Hawthorns Estate. As a hawthorn copse had apparently flourished at one time, it seemed an obvious and realistic choice of name, suggested by the then secretary Frank Heaven.

Initially, the ground housed 35,000 spectators and in 1902 the first of two FA Cup semi-finals was staged there when Derby County met Sheffield United. The second followed when Aston Villa met Wolverhampton Wanderers.

The freehold was purchased in 1913 for just £5,350 and shortly before the outbreak of the First World War the capacity had been increased to 48,500. The first section of concrete terracing was constructed in 1920, soon after Albion had won their first and only Football League Championship. In 1922 international football was first seen on Albion soil, when England played Ireland. Since then two other such matches have taken place at The Hawthorns: England versus Belgium in 1924 and England versus Wales in 1945.

From 1922 to 1923 the embankment on the Handsworth side of the ground was extended further back and the stand heightened, thus increasing the capacity even more. This led to the first 50,000-plus attendance being recorded when 56,474 fans attended the Albion versus Sunderland FA Cup-tie in February 1923. Two years later a crowd of 64,612 witnessed the Cup encounter with Aston Villa and this remained a ground record until March 1937 when it was bettered by just 203 – to a never-to-be-beaten 64,815 for the Albion versus Arsenal FA Cup quarter-final match.

Either side of the Second World War a lot of work was carried out at the ground, both internally and externally, reducing the capacity by a few thousand, and in 1954 the last 60,000-plus gate assembled at The Hawthorns for the Albion versus Newcastle United FA Cup-tie. Three years later floodlights were installed at a cost of £18,000. In 1964, after the wing section had been added to the main stand at the corner of Halfords Lane and the Birmingham Road, the Rainbow Stand was built on the Handsworth side of the ground, thus reducing the ground capacity by around 10,000 to 50,000.

In 1976/77 executive boxes were installed in the Rainbow Stand as well as a number of paddock seats, and between 1979 and 1982 the Halfords Lane stand was completely redeveloped. Several more executive boxes, seperate lounges for matchday sponsors and VIPs, and new facilities for the club's directors, the press and the players, manager, coaching staff and match officials were all introduced.

In 1985 the Smethwick End stand was re-roofed and soon afterwards plans were put into place to make The Hawthorns into an all-seater stadium. This objective was achieved and the ground was finally completed for the start of the 1996/97 season at a total cost amounting to £4.15 million.

In 1995 Albion had received over £2 million from the Football Trust towards the cost of redeveloping The Hawthorns and, in May 1998, record gate receipts of £270,000 were taken from the League game against Nottingham Forest.

Albion have now contested over 2,200 competitive games at The Hawthorns (including wartime fixtures) and the overall figure of matches played on the ground tops the 3,000 mark. Today, the capacity of the ground is set at just over 25,000 and the stadium itself is regarded as one of the best on the Nationwide circuit. It is certainly a ground befitting a Premier League club and when Albion do climb back into the top flight of English football, they can be sure of excellent support from their ardent and success-starved fans.

Over the last century, scores of great players have displayed their skills both for and against Albion. There have been many joyous occasions, several heart-breaking moments and so much to reflect upon regarding the ups and downs of West Bromwich Albion Football Club.

As time goes on there will, of course, be a lot more joy and despair for both players and supporters on and off the field. Hopefully, we shall witness the Baggies playing Premiership football at The Hawthorns.

Back in 1900/01 Albion were in the top flight (the old First Division). In 2000/01 – exactly 100 years later – let's pray we can get back there...

Enjoy the book...

Tony Matthews
July 2000

Three of West Bromwich Albion's five FA Cup final triumphs have come whilst the club has been at The Hawthorns. In 1953/54 the Baggies almost achieved the League and Cup double, finishing runners-up in the First Division to Wolverhampton Wanderers and winning the FA Cup at Wembley (beating Preston 3-2 in the final). This picture shows Albion's skipper Len Millard with the trophy and his delighted team-mates.

One

Early Days at the New Ground

The Hawthorns, situated on the border of Handsworth, Smethwick and West Bromwich, was officially opened on 3 September 1900 when Albion met Derby County in a First Division League game. A crowd of 20,104 saw the teams battle out a 1-1 draw. Steve Bloomer, the England international who was born in Cradley Heath, headed the first goal to give Derby the lead but Charlie 'Chippy' Simmons equalised ten minutes from time. This photograph was taken prior to kick-off and includes several Football League and FA officials and other distinguished guests. From left to right, back row: Mr I. Whitehouse (president of the Birmingham & District Football League), Mr W. Heath (Staffordshire FA secretary), Mr J. Campbell Orr (Birmingham FA secretary), Dr. I. Pitt (director), Mr T.H. Sidney (Football League vice-president), Mr H. Lockett (Football League secretary). Third row: Mr H. Powell (director), Mr T. Harris Spencer (director), Mr H. Radford (Football League committee), Mr C.E. Sutcliffe (Football League committee), Mr D. Haigh (Football League vice-president), Mr John J. Bentley (Football League president), Mr Harry Keys (chairman), Mr W.W. Hart (Football League committee), Mr W. McGregor (Football League founder), Mr C. Perry (director), Mr J. Lones (director). Second row (seated): Mr Frank Heaven (secretary), Mr C. Keys (auditor), Tom Pickering, Freddie Wheldon (captain), Charlie Simmons, Abe Jones, Archie Dunn, Amos Adams, Mr Jack Paddock (trainer). Front row (on ground): Mr J.M. Bayliss (director), John Chadburn, Dick Roberts, Joe Reader, Billy Williams, Harry Hadley. Alas, this wasn't to be a happy initial season for Albion at their new ground as they were relegated for the first time in their history, crashing into the Second Division with a meagre 22 points out of a possible 68.

Albion's first competitive goal at The Hawthorns was scored by twenty-two-year-old centre forward Charlie 'Chippy' Simmons in the League game against Derby County in September 1900. It was a well-struck shot from twelve yards following Abe Jones' precise pass. Simmons had two spells with Albion (1898-1904 and 1905-07). He scored 81 goals in 193 first-class matches and helped Albion win the Second Division championship in 1902. He was an England reserve, played in an international trial and also served with West Ham and Chesterfield. Simmons died in Wednesbury in 1937.

Inside forward Freddie Wheldon was thirty when he led Albion in the first game at The Hawthorns. An exceptionally fine footballer, he scored 82 goals in 129 games for Small Heath (now Birmingham City), 74 in 138 for Aston Villa and 3 in 29 for Albion. He also played for Portsmouth, QPR and Coventry. Wheldon starred in 4 full internationals for England, helped Blues win the Second Division title and gain promotion to the top flight in the early 1890s and then collected three League championship medals with Villa, also helping them complete the double in 1897. As a wicketkeeper for Worcestershire CCC (1899-1906) he scored almost 5,000 runs (including 3 centuries) and took 93 catches. Nicknamed 'Diamond', Wheldon was born in Langley Green, Oldbury, in 1869 and died in Worcester in 1924.

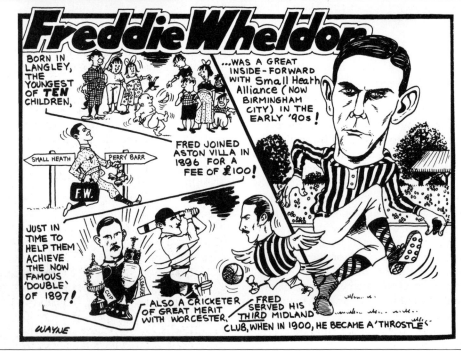

After such a disappointing first season at The Hawthorns, Albion's board of directors and management decided to gamble by securing the services of several new players (including some vastly experienced professionals) for the 1901/02 campaign. The gamble paid off and the Second Division championship was won in style with an impressive 55 points. Charlie Simmons, Tom Worton (ex-Wolves) and Billy Lee scored almost 60 goals between them and 8 players made more than 30 appearances during the season. Albion's championship-winning line-up was, from left to right, back row: Bill Brierley (trainer); Scotsman Jim Stevenson, formerly of Preston North End; West Bromwich-born Amos Adams; goalkeeper Ike Webb, signed from neighbours Small Heath; sturdy full-back Jack Kifford; Harry Hadley, who was to play for England in 1903. Middle row: Andrew Smith, a talented Scot from Stirlingshire; Billy Lee, who scored a goal every three games for Albion; captain Dan Nurse, who was secured from Molineux; in-form centre forward Charlie Simmons; Tom Worton, Nurse's team-mate from Wolves. Front row: wingers Jimmy McLean, the former Walsall player; George Dorsett, who went on to make 100 appearances for Albion before joining Manchester City.

Jack Kifford (with his back to the camera) tussles with Andrew 'Scottie' Smith during a training session at The Hawthorns in 1902. Kifford made almost 100 appearances for Albion in his four seasons with the club between 1901 and 1905. Born near Glasgow in 1878, he also played for Derby County, Bristol Rovers, Portsmouth, Millwall, Carlisle United and Coventry City and in 1903 was suspended by the Football Association for six weeks after being sent-off against Aston Villa. Utility forward Smith was born in 1879 and played for Stoke and Newton Heath (later to become Manchester United) before joining Albion and also appeared for Bristol Rovers, Millwall, Swindon Town and Leyton after leaving The Hawthorns. He spent three years with Albion – the longest period he ever stayed at one club.

This photograph, which was taken in 1905, shows the original main stand on the Halfords Lane side of The Hawthorns. Erected at the outset in 1900, it was to remain there for almost eighty years (with certain alterations being carried out over the course of time).

The pitch at The Hawthorns has always been described as one of the finest in the country. Here you see dedicated members of the Albion staff and volunteers from elsewhere carrying out repair work to the playing area during the early part of the twentieth century. Bill Barber (fourth from the left) was associated with the club for a total of twenty-six years, first as a reserve team player (1886-87), then as assistant trainer to his father-in-law Jack Paddock (1898-1905) and thereafter as head trainer (1905-22). It is believed that Barber scored the first goal for Albion's second XI at Baggott's Field, a ground the club used instead of Stoney Lane in bad weather.

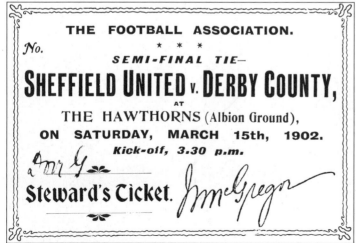

THE FOOTBALL ASSOCIATION.

* * *

No.

SEMI-FINAL TIE—

SHEFFIELD UNITED v. DERBY COUNTY,

AT

THE HAWTHORNS (Albion Ground),

ON SATURDAY, MARCH 15th, 1902.

Kick-off, 3.30 p.m.

Steward's Ticket.

In March 1902, the first of two FA Cup semi-finals was staged at The Hawthorns when Sheffield United met Derby County. The game ended in a 1-1 draw in front of an all-ticket crowd of 33,603. United went on to win the replay before going on to defeat Southampton in the final (again after a replay).

This page shows three pictures of Albion stalwart Jesse Pennington. Albion signed him as a nineteen-year-old from Dudley Town after he had been rejected by Aston Villa. He developed into the finest full-back of his generation, gaining 25 England caps (23 as partner to Blackburn's Bob Crompton). He appeared in almost 500 first-class games for the Baggies – a record that stood for more than fifty years until bettered by Tony Brown. Known as 'Peerless' Pennington, he skippered both club and country, and led Albion to the Second Division and First Division championships in 1911 and 1920 respectively, as well as playing in the beaten 1912 FA Cup final side. One of the 'cleanest' defenders of his time, he was perhaps at fault when Barnsley's Harry Tufnell scored the winning goal in that Cup Final replay as he allowed his opponent to streak clear when a challenge (even a foul) might have prevented the goal. Pennington played his first and last games for Albion against Liverpool and after retiring in 1922 he became coach at The Hawthorns. He died in Kidderminster in 1970, aged eighty-seven.

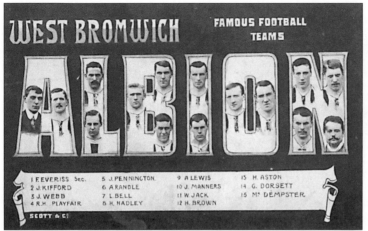

WEST BROMWICH
FAMOUS FOOTBALL TEAMS
ALBION

1 F. EVERISS Sec.	5 J. PENNINGTON	9 A LEWIS	13 H. ASTON
2 J. KIFFORD	6 A RANDLE	10 J. MANNERS	14 G. DORSETT
3 J. WEBB	7 L BELL	11 W JACK	15 M? DEMPSTER
4 R.H. PLAYFAIR	8 H. HADLEY	12 H. BROWN	

SCOTT & C?

Albion were relegated again at the end of the 1903/04 campaign. At the time there was very little money in the club's account and halfway through the next season home attendances fell below 3,000. Things went from bad to worse and on Bonfire Night 1904, a stand (Noah's Ark) which had been transferred from their old Stoney Lane ground burnt down. *Above*: Unfortunately 1904/05 wasn't a good season for Albion and they struggled, despite having some quality. Fred Everiss was secretary-manager, having replaced Frank Heaven in 1902. Jack Kifford, Ike Webb, Harry Hadley and George Dorsett had all helped Albion climb out of the Second Division in 1902. Full-back Jesse Pennington was now establishing himself in the team along with Arthur Randle, a quality right half, who moved to Leicester Fosse in 1908 but died four years later. Jack Manners played at centre half and left half while outside right Lawrie Bell, an FA Cup winner with Sheffield Wednesday in 1896, arrived from Brentford. His partner Walter Jack, a Scotsman, was signed from Bristol Rovers and centre forward Harry Brown, who was ex-Northampton Town, later played for Southampton, Fulham, Newcastle United and Bradford City. Wolverhampton-born inside left Albert Lewis scored a hat-trick on his Albion debut at Burnley in September 1904. Albion finished tenth in the Second Division, the average home gate was only 4,884 and then the whole board resigned. Harry Keys returned as chairman and ex-player Billy Bassett became a director. *Above right*: A typical advertisement from the early 1900s.

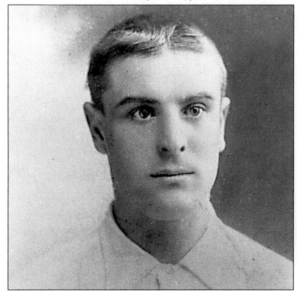

In November 1904 Albion signed centre half Ted 'Cock' Pheasant from Wolves. He was as tough as nails and went on to make over 150 appearances for Albion (scoring 22 goals) over the next six years before moving to Leicester Fosse. He died at the age of thirty-three.

Two
Second Division Champions

Harry Keys ('John Bull' to the players) was Albion's chairman during the torrid years between 1905 and 1908. Blunt and outspoken at times, he was once described by Fred Everiss as a 'man who called a spade a spade and sometimes a sanguinary shovel'. In 1905 he was elected to the Football League management committee and five years later became vice-president of the League, a position he held until his death in 1929. He was also an FA councillor and member of the international selection committee. Harry's two brothers were also very close to the Albion club (W. Hall was a director and Clement was a director and financial secretary/auditor) while his son, H. Wilson Keys, also became a director shortly after his father's death.

During the early part of the twentieth century a regular routine for the Albion players was to go for a brisk walk around the lanes and here you see trainer Bill Barber (third from the left) stepping out with a posse of first-teamers including Jack Manners, Charlie Simmons and Adam Haywood.

Left: In 1905 the club's first official matchday programme was produced. It comprised eight pages and was issued for the home League game with Burnley on 2 September of that year. Around 5,000 were printed and on the day a crowd of 7,223 saw the Baggies beaten 2-1 by their Lancashire opponents. *Right*: After playing for England at junior and senior levels, gaining both League championship and FA Cup winning medals with Aston Villa and having six very disappointing weeks with Leicester Fosse, thirty-year-old utility forward Billy Garraty moved to The Hawthorns in October 1908 for £270. Not a polished player by any means, he had guts and a never-say-die attitude and during his time with Albion scored 22 goals in 59 appearances, having previously netted 111 in 256 outings for Villa. On leaving The Hawthorns he joined Lincoln City and later became a lorry driver, delivering beer for Ansells Brewery.

Left: Press reports described Tommy Broad as being 'of the tearaway class, who runs like a greyhound'. He was quick but had a lot more to offer than just pace – he was a natural winger who, during a fine career, appeared in well over 350 senior games, scoring 35 goals. Born in Stalybridge, Broad, whose brother Jimmy also played professional football, joined Albion in September 1905 (after trials with Manchester City). He stayed at The Hawthorns until February 1908 during which time he netted once in 15 outings, injuries disrupting his performances considerably. However, on leaving Albion, Broad went on to play in turn for Chesterfield Town, Oldham Athletic, Bristol City, Manchester City, Stoke, Southampton and Rhyl, retiring in 1928. He was a junior international in 1906, represented the Football League XI and helped Oldham win promotion in 1910.

Centre: Full-back Amos Adams was a stylish footballer who made 214 senior appearances for Albion between 1897 and 1910. A local man, born in West Bromwich, he helped the Baggies win the Second Division championship in 1902 and one feels that if he had been with a more fashionable club (certainly one in the First Division) he would surely have represented England. After retiring just before the First World War, Adams became a sports master at a local school and in 1925 accepted a coaching position with the Amiens club in France. Later he became manager in season 1926/27.

Right: Welsh international Llewellyn Davies from Wrexham was the only player to oust the great Jesse Pennington from Albion's League side. After the Baggies had lost three consecutive Second Division matches – against Liverpool, Bristol City and Manchester United – Pennington was left out of the next match at home to Blackpool on 7 November 1904, with Davies taking over at left-back. Albion won 4-2. Davies played well and kept his place in the side but was moved to left-half, allowing Pennington to return to the side behind him. Davies, who won 13 caps in four different positions for his country, made only 3 appearances for the Baggies but amassed 379 for Wrexham, with whom he had four separate spells.

Left: The oldest player ever to don an Albion shirt in a competitive match is George Baddeley, who made his last appearance as a professional for the Baggies against Sheffield Wednesday on 18 April 1914 at the age of 39 years, 345 days. He is also one of the oldest players ever to line up in an FA Cup final, doing so for Albion against Barnsley two years earlier. Born in Stoke-on-Trent, right half Baddeley played in 225 games for Stoke before going to Albion for £250 in June 1908, where he played a further 157 games. He helped the Baggies win the Second Division championship in 1911.

Centre: Scorer of 48 goals in only 68 first team games for Albion, Wednesbury-born centre forward Fred Shinton had a never-say-die attitude. He was a wholehearted performer, who was robust, enthusiastic and simply loved hitting the back of the net. He rattled in three four-timers for Albion and in 1906/07 notched 28 goals in only 30 League matches. He spent just two-and-a-half years at The Hawthorns, from April 1905 to December 1907, before moving to Leicester Fosse. In fact, Albion struggled to find a ready replacement, using the likes of Billy Garraty, Fred Brown, Bill Jordan, Harry Wilcox and others – until Bob Pailor established himself in 1910.

Right: A native of Stockton-on-Tees, Bob Pailor played in the 1912 FA Cup final, having helped the Baggies win the Second Division championship the previous season. An out-and-out centre forward, he was aggressive, powerful and a prolific marksman, scoring a goal every two games for Albion (47 in 92 appearances). He was leading marksman in 1911/12 and 1912/13 before handing over to Alf Bentley. Signed from West Hartlepool in October 1908 at the age of twenty-one, he left The Hawthorns for Newcastle United in May 1914, making his debut for the Magpies against Albion four months later. Pailor retired prior to the the First World War with kidney trouble and opened a bookmakers business in the north-east. In later life he became blind and died in 1976, aged eighty-eight.

DEATH OF THE THROSTLE

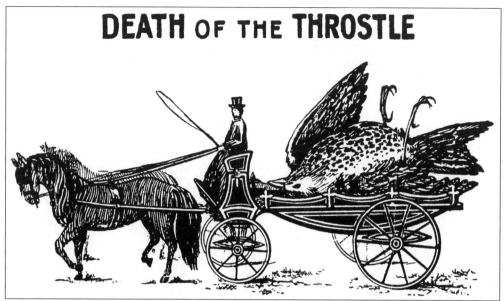

In 1906/07, Second Division Albion were knocked out of the FA Cup by Everton from the First Division at the semi-final stage. This cartoon drawing depicts their demise. In their three earlier round matches Albion had knocked out Norwich City (1-0), Derby County (2-0) and Notts County (3-1) all at The Hawthorns. However, at neutral Burnden Park, the home of Bolton Wanderers, they were defeated 2-1 by the Merseysiders in front of 32,381 spectators. Everton went on to lose 2-1 to Sheffield Wednesday in the final.

Albion's line-up at the start of the 1910/11 season for the away game at Bolton Wanderers on 5 September. From left to right, back row: A. Evans (coach), E. Paddock (assistant trainer), S. Timmins, A. Richards, H. Pearson, R. Pailor, F. Everiss (secretary-manager), G. Baddeley, J. Manners, D. Nurse (director). Middle row: W. Barber (trainer), W. Wollaston, F. Buck, J. Smith, F. Waterhouse. Front row: S. Bowser, A. Lloyd. Inset: B. Shearman, J. Pennington, J. Nevin. Albion had a terrific season, winning the Second Division title – but only after a last match 1-0 home victory over Huddersfield Town, Fred Buck netting the all-important goal from the penalty spot after half-an-hour's play.

In the 1911/12 season, Albion reached their sixth FA Cup final, having knocked out Tottenham Hotspur, Leeds City, Sunderland, Fulham and Blackburn Rovers. They were marked up as favourites to beat Second Division Barnsley in the final at Crystal Palace but things didn't work out according to plan. The initial game ended goalless after extra-time in front of 55,213 fans. The replay, at Bramall Lane (cycling distance from Barnsley), attracted a crowd of 38,555 (30,000 cheering on the Tykes) and again the match went into extra-time before Harry Tufnell broke Albion's hearts by scoring the only goal of the game in the 119th minute! These two newspaper photographs from the first encounter at Crystal Palace show Albion attacking the Barnsley goal (above) and Claude Jephcott (striped shirt) trying to burst into the Barnsley penalty area (below).

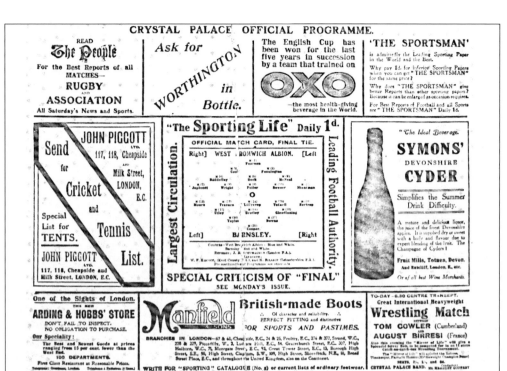

Programme from the initial 1912 FA Cup final at the Crystal Palace.

Left: A postcard featuring a song for Albion supporters at the 1912 Cup Final. *Right*: A ticket for a dinner at The Dartmouth Hotel, commemorating Albion's appearance in the 1912 final.

Left: Goalkeeper Hubert Pearson punches clear during a League game against Newcastle United in February 1912. Pearson made 377 first team appearances for Albion and actually scored two goals (both penalties). He was nineteen years of age when he joined The Hawthorns' professional ranks in February 1906 and, after taking over the green jersey from Jimmy Stringer four years later, he was first choice between the posts for virtually the whole of the next twelve years before George Ashmore assumed command. A junior international, Pearson was chosen for the full international between England and France in 1923 but was forced to miss the game through injury and never got another chance. His son Harold took over the mantle of Albion goalkeeper from 1927 until 1937.

Centre: Sid Bowser was a gritty footballer, who was tough and dedicated. Born in Handsworth, he joined Albion in July 1908 as a forward and stayed for five years before signing for the Irish club Distillery. He returned to The Hawthorns in February 1914 as a mature, confident centre half and remained a force in the side until joining Walsall ten years later, having appeared in a total of 371 first-class games for the Baggies (with 71 goals to his credit). He played in Albion's Second Division and First Division championship winning sides of 1911 and 1920 respectively, lined up in the 1912 FA Cup final and won an England cap against Ireland in 1919. A genuine sportsman who loved his football, Bowser later became a publican in Dudley and spent twenty-five years in the licensing trade before his death in 1961, aged sixty-nine.

Right: Fred Morris, Tipton born and bred, was the first player to score 100 League goals for Albion, reaching that milestone in November 1922 with his last kick of the game against Manchester City at The Hawthorns to seal a 2-0 win. Morris had joined Albion eleven years earlier and in 1919/20 netted a record 37 goals when the First Division championship came to West Bromwich. A terrific marksman, strongly built, courageous, exciting and most of all a wonderful opportunist, he formed a marvellous left-wing partnership with Howard Gregory. He left Albion for Coventry City in 1924 having secured 118 goals in 287 senior appearances for the Baggies. Morris, capped twice by England, also played for the Football Association XI and Football League sides. He died in Great Bridge in 1962, aged sixty-eight.

Howard Gregory was Fred Morris' enterprising left-wing partner at The Hawthorns for five seasons (1919/20 to 1923/24). Ginger-haired, fast and tricky with a powerful shot in either foot, Gregory – a native of Aston – arrived at Albion during the same week as Morris in May 1911 and both players made their senior debuts for the club in April 1924, Gregory's coming nine days after his colleague's. They became bosum friends and teased and tormented defenders left, right and centre. Gregory went on to score 45 goals in 181 appearances for the club before retiring in 1926. He was a key figure in the 1920 League Championship-winning side, serving up chances galore for Morris! Gregory died in Birmingham in 1954, aged sixty-one.

After reaching the FA Cup final the previous season, Albion finished a disappointing tenth in the First Division in 1912/13, but to a certain degree this was the time when several players were either coming to the end of their respective careers while others were just beginning to establish themselves in the first eleven. There were, in fact, well over thirty professionals on the pay-roll and this photograph was taken before the start of a pre-season friendly (the stripes against the whites) at The Hawthorns. The line-up consists of, from left to right, back row: A. Lloyd, J. Steer, L. Moorwood, G. Snead, J. Varty, M. Wood, C. Crutchley, B. Millward, S. Jones, A. Graham, J. Mann. Second row: E. Smith (assistant secretary), T. Fletcher, G. Baddeley, H. Pearson, S. Bowser, J. Manners, Mr W.I. Bassett (chairman), F. Waterhouse, C. Deacey, R. Pailor, F. Morris, H. Lane, Mr F. Everiss (secretary). Third row: Mr D. Nurse (director), A. Cook, Mr H. Keys (director), J. Pennington, R. McNeal, Sir E. J. Spencer (president), F. Buck, W. Barber (trainer). Front row: C. Jephcott, W. Jackson, B. Shearman, J. Smith, H. Wright, J. Smart, J. Donald, H. Gregory.

This photograph, taken from near the players' tunnel on the Halfords Lane side of The Hawthorns, shows a goal being scored by Albion's Ben Shearman during the First Division League game against Liverpool in September 1912. A crowd of almost 22,000 saw the Baggies win 3-1.

The winter of 1914 was a bitterly cold one with the West Midlands taking the brunt of the arctic conditions. These photographs show snow covering the Birmingham Road end terraces and the pitch (above) and the club officials wrapped up warmly (left), one of them being former player and then director Charlie Perry (in the centre).

Three
Champions

For the first and only time in the club's history, West Bromwich Albion won the Football League championship in 1919/20. They did so in style, setting many records during the course of the campaign. The Baggies won the star prize by attaining 60 points from 28 wins and 4 draws with just 10 defeats, scoring 104 goals (Fred Morris weighing in with 37) and conceding 47. Notts County were hammered 8-0 at home (Morris netting five times) and four or more goals were claimed on fifteen occasions. Albion's average home League attendance was an impressive 30,532 – almost 20,000 higher than that of the last pre-war League season of 1914/15 and better than the previous best by almost 10,000. From left to right, back row: Mr W. Barber (trainer), H. Pearson, Mr W. Gopsill (masseur), Mr E. Smith (assistant secretary). Second row: Mr F. Everiss (secretary), Mr D. Nurse (director), A. Cook, Mr W.I. Bassett (vice-chairman), Mr H. Keys (chairman), C. Jephcott, Mr A. Seymour (director), M.C. Perry (director). Third row: J. Crisp, A.W. Smith, R. McNeal, J. Pennington, S. Bowser, F. Morris, H. Gregory. Front row: J. Smith, T. Magee, A. Bentley, S. Richardson.

At a fraction over 5ft 2in tall, Tommy Magee is reputed to be the smallest player ever to appear for England in a full international match or to don an Albion shirt at senior level. He joined the club whilst serving in the trenches in occupied France in January 1919 and lined up in a handful of wartime games before embarking on his senior career with the Baggies in September 1919, making the first of his 434 appearances for the club in a 3-1 home win over Oldham Athletic which set Albion on course for the League championship. Magee first played at inside right, but after having a spell on the right-wing, he finally settled down as a gritty, hard-tackling, tenacious right half. The only Albion player to gain both League and FA Cup winners' medals, he won the latter in 1931 when Birmingham were defeated 2-1 at Wembley. He also played 5 times for England and twice toured Canada with the FA in 1926 and 1931. A 'pocket Hercules' he spent fifteen years at The Hawthorns before leaving to join Crystal Palace. He died in May 1974, aged seventy-five.

Joe Smith was a superb right-back who served Albion for sixteen years (1910 to 1926), amassing 471 appearances. He won both Second and First Division championship medals (in 1911 and 1920 respectively) but missed the 1912 FA Cup final through injury. He formed a marvellous partnership with Jesse Pennington and later with Billy Adams and Arthur Perry, achieving a remarkable level of consistency (illustrated by the fact that he missed only 5 League games out of a possible 252 between 1919 and 1925). A fine positional player with good technique, he played 3 times for England in one victory international and two senior fixtures against Ireland in 1919 and 1922. On leaving Albion, Smith joined Birmingham and later became a licensee. He died in Wolverhampton in 1956, aged sixty-six.

Left: Another key member of Albion's League Championship-winning team of 1919/20 was left half Bobby McNeal – the steel in the side. Born in the North East, he joined Albion in June 1910 and remained a player at the Hawthorns for fifteen years, amassing 403 senior appearances and scoring 10 goals. He had a footballing brain, defended well and distributed the ball efficiently. He played behind Fred Morris and Howard Gregory and in front of Jesse Pennington – making Albion's left-hand side the strongest in the seasons immediately after the First World War. Capped by England on two occasions, McNeal also represented the Football League and played for Albion in their Second Division championship-winning side of 1910/11 and in the 1912 FA Cup final. He died in Durham in May 1956, aged sixty-five.

Centre: As a replacement for Alf Bentley and a strike partner to Fred Morris, Albion recruited the services of Bobby Blood from Port Vale for a record fee of £4,000 in February 1921. The twenty-five year old from Harpur Hill near Buxton had already shown his worth by scoring 44 goals in only 53 League outings for the Vale, having previously rattled in no fewer than 400 in eight seasons with Leek Town – including 105 in two wartime campaigns between 1917 and 1919. Blood overcame two serious injuries while serving in the army and developed into one of the most prolific marksmen in the country, despite having one leg shorter than the other! He went on to net 26 goals in 53 outings for Albion before moving to Stockport County. Blood played – and scored – until he was well past his thirty-seventh birthday. Not the tallest of players (he was only 5ft 7in), he battled bravely and had the knack of being in the right place at the right time. He died in Buxton in August 1988, aged ninety-four.

Right: Wing half Reg Fryer made 21 appearances for Albion during the 1920s. Born in Birmingham in 1904, he joined the club's professional ranks in 1924 but had to battle hard and long to get a first team outing. However, he remained loyal to the club for six years before joining Shrewsbury Town in 1930.

In 1925, The Hawthorns was one of the largest grounds in the country with a capacity of 65,000 – this rose to 70,000 soon afterwards, although the record attendance at the ground was set some years later when 64,815 spectators witnessed the Albion v. Arsenal FA Cup quarter-final clash in March 1937. In fact, the 60,000 mark has only been topped on four occasions – 1954 being the last time when Albion met Newcastle United in a fifth round FA Cup-tie. The agreed capacity of the stadium in the year 2000 was almost 26,000.

West Bromwich Albion Football Club, Ltd.

Telephone, 95 West Bromwich.
Telegraphic Address, Football, Westbromwich.

Registered Office and Ground,
The Hawthorns, Birmingham Road,
West Bromwich.

Date as Postmark.

Dear Sir,

You are selected to play v. *Aston Villa*

at *Aston* on *tomorrow* Sat next, *Oct 15* Kick-off *3 pm*

...................................leaves...................................at...................................

Kindly be punctual and oblige,

Good luck

Yours truly,

FRED EVERISS,
Secretary.

A postcard sent to centre forward Bobby Blood at his home in Harpur Hill informing him that he had been selected to play for Albion against Aston Villa (away) on Saturday 15 October 1921. A crowd of 58,000 saw Albion win 1-0, the goalscorer none other than Bobby Blood himself.

Fred Morris (not in picture) scored this stunning goal for Albion against the famous Corinthians in an FA Cup second round tie at The Hawthorns in February 1924. A crowd of over 49,000 saw Albion win 5-0. This was the last of Morris' 118 goals for the Baggies before he left to join Coventry City.

Left: Full-back Dicky Baugh's father (who had the same name) appeared for Wolves in three FA Cup finals between 1889 and 1896 and he also played twice for England. Baugh junior certainly wanted to follow in his father's footsteps as he too served with the Wolves. However, it was not to be as he was forced to miss the 1921 Cup Final through injury. After being induced by an agent to join Cardiff City, Baugh was fined and severely censored by a joint FA/Welsh committee, yet went on to make 120 appearances for the Molineux club before transferring to The Hawthorns for £500 in June 1924, initially as cover for Arthur Perry. He starred in 65 senior games for Albion, being a regular in the side from February 1925 to November 1926. Then George Shaw arrived on the scene, followed by Bob Finch and all of a sudden Albion were well blessed with full-backs. This led to Baugh leaving the club to join Exeter City in the summer of 1929. *Right*: Fred Reed was a tough tackling, no-nonsense centre half. A native of the North-East, he moved to join the Albion as a professional in February 1913. Reed acted as reserve to first Fred Buck and then Sid Bowser before establishing himself in the Baggies' League side halfway through the 1921/22 campaign. He became club skipper and went on to make well over 150 senior appearances for the club (with 5 goals) before handing over the pivotal role to Ted Rooke in 1927. On retiring, Reed was appointed trainer at The Hawthorns, a position he held with pride until 1950. He died in West Bromwich in December 1967, aged seventy-three.

Left: Harry Chambers, an English international, was thirty-one when he joined Albion in March 1928 after scoring over 150 goals for Liverpool. An inside forward, he started off in this position with the Baggies but later moved back to centre half before leaving The Hawthorns with just 46 games under his belt. *Right*: Inside right Ivor Jones was capped 10 times by Wales. He joined Albion from Swansea Town in April 1922 and made 67 appearances for the Baggies (scoring 10 goals) before switching his allegiance back to the Vetch Field. His son, Cliff Jones, starred for Spurs during the 1960s.

Left: Stan Davies could play anywhere – and did! Capped 18 times by Wales, he also toured Canada with the FAW party in 1929 and played in six different positions for his country, once taking over in goal, such was his determination to play football. A former coalminer, he spent six years with Albion (1921 to 1927) and scored 83 goals in 159 appearances before moving to Birmingham. During his career Davies also assisted, among others, Rochdale, Preston, Everton, Cardiff City, Rotherham United and Barnsley. He was seventy-four when he died in Birmingham in 1972. *Right*: Joe Carter played with Jones, Chambers and Davies in Albion's forward line, but it was as partner to outside right Tommy Glidden that he was most effective. A native of Aston, Carter joined Albion in 1921 and remained at The Hawthorns until 1936. During that time he scored 155 goals in 451 appearances, helped Albion complete the FA Cup and promotion double in 1931, lined up in the 1935 FA Cup final and won 3 England caps. He also played for Tranmere, Walsall and Sheffield Wednesday (briefly). Carter later became a licensee in Handsworth where he died in 1977, aged seventy-five.

Down the years League and Cup clashes between Aston Villa and Albion have always been well contested and to date almost 150 competitive matches have taken place with the Baggies chalking up 50 wins to Villa's 68. The picture here shows Albion under pressure during a game at Villa Park in the 1920s when the crowds at both grounds were practically full. In fact, in season 1924/25 the teams met four times (twice in the League, twice in the FA Cup) and the aggregate attendance figure was a staggering 194,876 (an average of 48,719) – this included a midweek afternoon game and one played in heavy rain!

Jimmy Spencer was a small but quick, energetic outside right who scored 3 goals in 66 first-class games for Albion between 1922 and 1927. A Yorkshireman, he was on the brink of international honours after representing the Football League and playing in the Professional Select XI in 1924, but injuries prevented him from gaining a full cap. He contested the right-wing berth with Tommy Glidden following the departure of Jack Crisp. Spencer joined Villa (as a reserve) on leaving The Hawthorns.

West Bromwich Albion F. C.
1926 – 27.

(a set of player autographs, including:)
T. L. Wilkinson, Wm Adams, S. Davies, H. Smith, J. H. Carter, S. Richardson, R Baugh, J. E. Byers, H. P. Dutton, Geo James, Ed Brooke, J. S. Short, G. S. Ashmore, N Howarth, J Spooner, H W Reed, G Ed Shaw, G. A. Titterton, W Ashurst, Jos Glidden, R. McNeal, W Hudson, E Heckman, J. Magee, Phil Hunt

A set of authentic autographs of Albion players and other Hawthorns' officials from 1926/27 – not one of the club's greatest seasons as they were relegated to the Second Division!

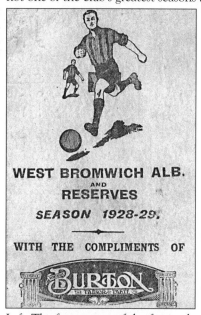

WEST BROMWICH ALB.
AND
RESERVES

SEASON 1928-29.

WITH THE COMPLIMENTS OF

BURTON

Left: The front cover of the fixture list for the 1928/29 campaign. *Right*: Jimmy Cookson started with a bang after joining Albion for £2,500 in June 1927, setting a new club record in his first season at The Hawthorns with 38 Second Division goals and reaching the milestone of 100 League goals in only 89 matches. Cookson's record with Albion was tremendous – 110 goals in only 131 first-class outings. He left The Hawthorns in August 1933 to join Plymouth Argyle. It was amazing he never gained an England cap – his only representative honours came with the FA XI on tour to Canada in 1931. He died in Warminster in December 1970, aged sixty-six.

Four

The Double, W.G. Richardson and Relegation

With his mud-splattered team-mates alongside him, Albion captain Tommy Glidden heads towards the tunnel, clutching the FA Cup after Birmingham had been defeated 2-1 in the 1931 FA Cup final at Wembley in front of 90,368 spectators.

In 1929/30 Albion scored a club record 105 Second Division goals, with Tommy Glidden, Joe Carter and Jimmy Cookson amassing 72 between them. Another player, W.G. Richardson, weighed in with a modest 2 goals. However, during the following season it was 'W.G.' himself who stole the limelight, taking Cookson's place and helping Albion complete a unique double: that of gaining promotion from the Second Division and winning the FA Cup – a feat never achieved before or since. 'W.G.' scored 18 League goals and 6 in the FA Cup, including both against Blues in the FA Cup final. Albion powered through to Wembley by beating Charlton Athletic (at the third attempt), Tottenham Hotspur, Portsmouth, neighbours Wolves (after a replay) and Everton in the semi-final at Old Trafford in front of 69,241 fans. The team was practically the same throughout the campaign: Harold Pearson; George Shaw, Bert Trentham; Tommy Magee, Bill Richardson, Jimmy Edwards; Tommy Glidden, Joe Carter, Teddy Sandford, Stan Wood. All of these players were Englishmen. *Above*: The Albion players take the field at Wembley. *Below*: The team are introduced to HRH the Duke of Gloucester, with Jimmy 'Iron' Edwards prominent as he shakes hands with the Prince.

Early first half action from the 1931 FA Cup final taken from a W.D. & H.O. Wills cigarette card series entitled 'Home Events'. Albion are playing from left to right.

Albion's first ever goal at Wembley arrived in the twenty-fifth minute courtesy of ace centre forward W.G. Richardson (positioned just beyond the six-yard line behind team-mate Stan Wood). The Blues 'keeper is England international Harry Hibbs.

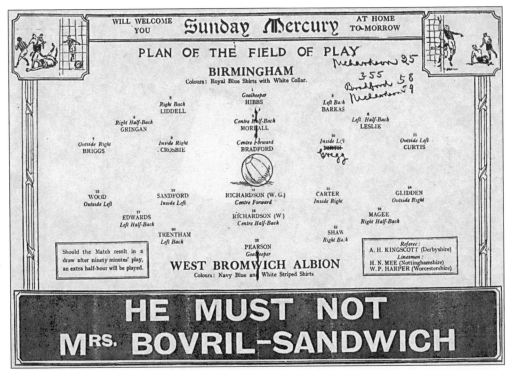

PLAN OF THE FIELD OF PLAY

BIRMINGHAM
Colours: Royal Blue Shirts with White Collar.

Richardson 25
355
Bradford 58
Richardson 59

1
Goalkeeper
HIBBS

2
Right Back
LIDDELL

3
Left Back
BARKAS

4
Right Half-Back
GRINGAN

5
Centre Half-Back
MORRALL

6
Left Half-Back
LESLIE

7
Outside Right
BRIGGS

8
Inside Right
CROSBIE

9
Centre Forward
BRADFORD

10
Inside Left
Gregg

11
Outside Left
CURTIS

12
WOOD
Outside Left

13
SANDFORD
Inside Left

14
RICHARDSON (W. G.)
Centre Forward

15
CARTER
Inside Right

16
GLIDDEN
Outside Right

17
EDWARDS
Left Half-Back

18
RICHARDSON (W.)
Centre Half-Back

19
MAGEE
Right Half-Back

20
TRENTHAM
Left Back

21
SHAW
Right Back

22
PEARSON
Goalkeeper

WEST BROMWICH ALBION
Colours: Navy Blue and White Striped Shirts

Should the Match result in a draw after ninety minutes' play, an extra half-hour will be played.

Referee:
A. H. KINGSCOTT (Derbyshire)
Linesmen :
H. N. MEE (Nottinghamshire)
W. P. HARPER (Worcestershire)

How the teams lined up in the 1931 FA Cup final.

Thousands of supporters greeted Albion when they returned to West Bromwich with the trophy. Here, skipper Tommy Glidden shows off the silver prize on board a local corporation bus.

As FA Cup holders, Albion were invited to take the trophy everywhere and often did – even down a mine in Cheshire!

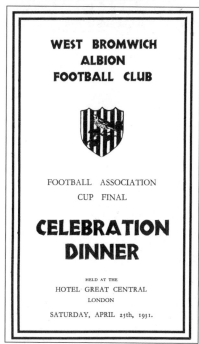

Left: The Albion players, directors and other staff attended a special celebration dinner in London's Hotel Great Central on the evening of their FA Cup final triumph with their wives and girlfriends.
Right: Harold Pearson, son of Hubert who played for the club from 1906 to 1926, was one of the country's finest goalkeepers during the early 1930s and played for England against Scotland in 1932. He spent twelve years with Albion (1925 to 1937) and appeared in 303 first-class games, collecting an FA Cup winners' medal in 1931 as well as helping the team gain promotion from the Second Division. Born in Tamworth and nicknamed 'Algy', Pearson died in November 1994, aged eighty-six.

Left: Centre forward Billy Richardson was given the initials 'W.G.' to distinguish himself from another player of the same name who was in the Albion side at the same time. On his day he had few equals and certainly no superiors at snapping up the half chance. A truly great goalscorer, he was quick, assertive, penetrative and a deadly finisher. He joined Albion from Hartlepools United in June 1929 for just £1,250. Over the next ten years he scored 228 League and FA Cup goals for the Baggies in 354 games and then during the Second World War added another 100 to his tally. He bagged 55 goals for Shrewsbury in 1945/46 and in all matches as a professional scored well over 450 goals, including 50 in his first season of Central League football (1929/30). A magnificent striker, 'W.G.' netted both Albion's goals in their FA Cup final triumph over Birmingham in 1931 and then headed the winning goal at home to Charlton a week later that clinched promotion from the Second Division. On retiring he became a coach at The Hawthorns but sadly died when playing in a charity match in 1959, aged forty-nine. *Right*: Teddy Sandford made his debut for Albion in November 1930 and was still only twenty when he helped the Baggies beat Birmingham in the FA Cup final the following April. A strong, resourceful footballer, he was always involved in the action and possessed a powerful shot with both feet. Sandford started out as an inside left before moving to centre half, where he played as the team's captain. He made 317 appearances for Albion, scored 75 goals and was capped once by England (against Wales in 1932). On leaving The Hawthorns in 1939, he had a brief spell with Sheffield United and later returned to Albion as a coach and scout. He died in Birmingham in 1995.

Above: Tommy Glidden, seen here leading out the team followed by W.G. Richardson, served Albion for over fifty years – initially as a player (1922-36), then coach, prominent shareholder and finally club director (1951-74). Born near Newcastle in 1902 and a former amateur with Sunderland, he began his career at inside right but developed into a brilliant goalscoring right-winger. He made 479 appearances for Albion (445 in the League) and claimed 140 goals. He led the Baggies to victory in the 1931 FA Cup final, skippered the side again in the 1935 Cup Final and was certainly unlucky not to win a full England cap. He died of a heart attack in July 1974, aged seventy-two.
Right: Wally 'Titty' Boyes was initially an outside left – who once scored 17 goals in a schoolboy match in Sheffield before joining Albion in February 1931. He took over from Stan Wood on the left flank and scored in the 1935 FA Cup final before switching to left-half as well as occupying the inside left berth at times. After appearing in 165 senior matches for the Baggies, scoring 38 goals, he was transferred to Everton in 1938. He gained a League Championship medal in his first season at Goodison Park and took his total number of England caps up to 4. Boyes retired as a player in 1953 and died in September 1960, aged forty-seven.

In November 1931 Albion travelled to London to play West Ham United in a First Division League game. Spectators were still entering the ground when W.G. Richardson fired Albion into a fifth minute lead. Two minutes later 'W.G.' scored again and he duly completed his hat-trick 50 seconds later with fans still taking up their positions! With just nine minutes gone it was 4-0 to the Baggies with Richardson again on target. Four goals in four or five minutes (reporters differed in opinion regarding the timing) meant that the Albion centre forward had equalled the all-time record for rapid scoring set by Jim McIntyre of Blackburn Rovers against Everton nine years earlier. Albion eventually won the match 5-1 – and at least 2,000 of the 18,134 spectators missed at least two and perhaps three of the goals! Some may even have missed the Hammers' consolation effort as Albion were leading 5-0 at the time! The picture here shows Richardson's third goal flying in past Hammers' 'keeper Ted Hufton.

This is the cover of a typical Albion matchday programme from the 1930s. The production comprised twelve pages with advertisements on at least four of them. The statistics (fixtures, results, line-ups, tables) appeared on pages five and nine and the team line-ups on page ten. The cover price was two old pence and it is believed that on average 5,000 copies were printed for each home game (with 6,500-7,000 for major cup matches).

During the 1930s, Albion often got the better of Chelsea in League games. Of the fourteen First Division encounters between 1931 and 1938, Albion won eight and drew three. This picture shows centre forward W.G. Richardson (left, with arms raised) celebrating after scoring at Stamford Bridge in Albion's 2-1 victory in March 1933. Walter Robbins is the other Albion player in shot.

Left: Action from the Chelsea *v.* Albion League game at Stamford Bridge in March 1934. The Baggies lost a five-goal thriller 3-2 in front of almost 21,000 fans. The photograph shows W.G. Richardson being thwarted by the Chelsea 'keeper Vic Woodley. *Right*: Right half Jimmy Murphy took over from Tommy Magee in Albion's first team in 1932/33 and went on to make 223 first team appearances before leaving The Hawthorns for Swindon Town in 1939. Born in Ton Petre, South Wales, Murphy was a very competitive player who joined Albion in 1928. He played in the 1935 FA Cup final defeat by Sheffield Wednesday and gained 15 caps for his country. He was appointed coach at Old Trafford in 1945 and, following the Munich air crash in 1958, he took over from Matt Busby as caretaker-manager of Manchester United. He also managed the Welsh national team between 1956 and 1963, taking them to the 1958 World Cup finals. Murphy died in Manchester on 14 November 1989, aged eighty-one.

In 1934/35, Albion reached their second FA Cup final in four years. En route the Baggies had knocked out Port Vale (2-1), Sheffield United (7-1), Stockport County (5-0), Preston North End (1-0) and Bolton Wanderers (2-0 after a 1-1 draw). The deciding goal against Preston, shown here, was scored by Arthur Gale, who was deputising for skipper Tommy Glidden.

Unfortunately, this time they weren't as lucky as they had been in 1931. Coming up against a strong Sheffield Wednesday side, they were beaten 4-2, the last two Owls' goals coming late in the game after Albion had twice equalised through Walter Boyes and Teddy Sandford. At 2-2 Albion should have gone ahead, but the usually reliable W.G. Richardson missed a sitter when it looked easier to score. *Left*: Albion's 1935 FA Cup final line-up. *Right*: A match ticket for the Cup Final.

Albion's first equalising goal against Sheffield Wednesday in the 1935 FA Cup final. Walter Boyes (not in picture) was the scorer.

Albion goalkeeper Harold Pearson collects a high centre during the 1935 Cup Final, with Sheffield Wednesday's captain Ronnie Starling about to pounce. Jimmy Murphy is the player looking on.

Albion's second XI ('The Stiffs') won the Central League championship three seasons in succession: 1932/33, 1933/34 and 1934/35. Over that period they played 126 matches, won 82, drew 20 and lost only 24. They scored a staggering 328 goals and conceded 168, amassing 184 points. The mainstays of the team during the three campaigns were full-backs Bob Finch, who went on to appear in 231 reserve team games for the club, and Hugh Foulkes; utility forward Arthur Gale, who scored 39 goals in 1933/34 and 41 the following season (he netted 146 for the second XI all told); goalkeeper Ted Crowe; defenders Alf Ridyard and 'Bos' Trevis; Welshman Walter Robbins; former Huddersfield Town star Harry Raw; and local man Jack Rix. In March 1934, a record attendance for a Central League game at The Hawthorns (22,372) witnessed the 2-2 draw between Albion and Aston Villa.

In October 1935 Albion beat Aston Villa 7-0 on their own patch in front of a 38,000 plus crowd. W.G. Richardson (four), Stan Wood, Jack Mahon and Jack Sankey were the scorers. This is Albion's best-ever win (League or cup) over the Villa who were relegated to the Second Division for the first time in the club's history at the end of the season.

On the last day of the 1935/36 season, Albion travelled to St Andrew's to play Birmingham. A crowd of 28,124 saw the Baggies win 3-1 – Walter Boyes pictured here scoring the decisive third goal past Harry Hibbs, the England 'keeper.

In 1937 Albion were just one game away from reaching their third FA Cup final in seven years. After eliminating Spennymoor United (7-1), Darlington (3-2), Coventry City (3-2) and Arsenal (3-1 in front of a record Hawthorns crowd of 64,815), they met Preston North End at Highbury – three days after the death of club chairman and former player Billy Bassett. Bassett's death, one feels, clearly affected the team and on the day they were second best to Preston who won comfortably by 4-1 in front of a near 43,000 crowd. *Above*: Both teams wore black armbands and a minute's silence took place before kick-off. *Below*: Walter Boyes, the Albion left-winger, getting in a cross during the semi-final at Highbury.

As founder members of the Football League in 1888, both Albion and Bolton Wanderers have always been keen rivals out on the pitch. In 1936/37 the Wanderers got the better of the Baggies in both matches, winning 2-0 at The Hawthorns and 4-1 at Burnden Park. This picture shows Albion goalkeeper Harold Pearson punching clear from Joe Milsom as Bolton attack the Smethwick End in the game at The Hawthorns on 14 November.

Albion forward Harry Jones gets in a shot in a home game against Grimsby in 1937. Albion were relegated to the Second Division in 1937/38. They fought long and hard during the campaign but in the end their leaky defence let them down as 91 goals were conceded. Albion lost their last three matches – all away from home – when a win and a draw would have saved them.

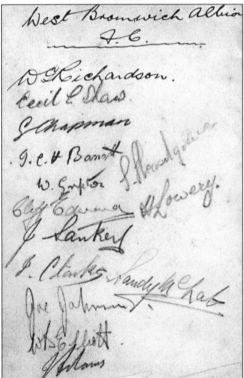

Above left: On 20 August 1938, to celebrate the Football League Jubilee, Albion visited arch rivals Aston Villa in a pre-season friendly. A crowd of 26,640 witnessed a 1-1 draw, with Harry Jones scoring for the Baggies. Twelve months later the teams played out another 1-1 draw in front of 16,007 fans. This is the cover of the programme issued for the 1938 game. *Above right*: Before joining Albion in March 1938, pint-sized left half Sandy McNab played in over 100 games for Sunderland, helping them win the Championship and the FA Cup. A marvellously gifted footballer, he served Albion for eight years, making 181 first team appearances (131 of them during the war) and skippering the side on many occasions. He won 2 Scottish caps, represented the Football League and toured Canada and the USA with the Scottish FA in 1939. McNab died in September 1962, aged fifty. *Left*: Albion players' autographs from 1938/39.

Five

Wartime, Promotion and Two Irishmen

In May 1946 Albion secretary Fred Everiss and director Claude Jephcott travelled over to Ireland to sign centre forward Dave Walsh from Linfield for £3,500 – a straight replacement for W.G. Richardson. The picture shows Everiss welcoming his new goalscorer to The Hawthorns.

Action from the Walsall *v.* Albion Midland Regional wartime fixture at Fellows Park in March 1940. The game ended in a 1-1 draw.

Left: Peter 'Ma-Ba' McKennan was a well-built, hard-shooting, Scottish-born inside forward who, as a guest, scored a hat-trick on his debut for Albion in a 7-2 win over Northampton Town in December 1941. McKennan also played for Partick Thistle, Leicester City, Brentford, Middlesbrough and Oldham Athletic. He netted 17 goals in 27 games for Albion during and after the war. He helped Oldham win the Third Division (North) title in 1953 and also twice represented the Scottish League whilst with Partick. *Right*: Dave Walsh, now resident in Devon, had scored 122 goals in Irish football before joining Albion in 1946. He added another 100 to his tally with the Baggies before moving across to nearby Aston Villa in 1950 and then on to Walsall. He was capped 31 times at full international level (for both Irelands). Walsh was born in Waterford in 1924 and helped Albion win promotion from the Second Division in 1949, having earlier won League and cup medals with Linfield.

In 1946, the players and officials of West Bromwich Albion Football Club were invited to attend an ice hockey match at the Sports Stadium, Brighton. *Above*: Albion players enjoying the action, from left to right: Frank Hodgetts, Dennis Gordon, Arthur Rowley, Alun Evans, Len Millard, Billy Elliott, Norman Heath, Harry Kinsell, Jim Pemberton, George Drury. *Below*: A few of the players join forces with members of the host club, Brighton Tigers, for an informal team photograph.

Irish international centre half Jack Vernon spent five years with Albion (1947 to 1952) during which time he appeared in exactly 200 senior games. He won 22 caps and represented Great Britain against the Rest of Europe in 1947 and skippered the United Kingdom XI *v.* Wales in 1951.

Norman Heath, the Albion goalkeeper, handles the ball safely during a Second Division game at Tottenham in December 1947.

Albion team photograph taken in 1948. From left to right, back row: Arthur Smith, signed from Leicester City for £5,000; Len Millard, who made well over 600 appearances for the club; goalkeeper Jim Sanders, a 1945 signing from Charlton Athletic; Jim Pemberton from Wolverhampton; Ray Barlow, a brilliant footballer who starred in 482 games for the Baggies between 1944 and 1960; half-back Glyn Hood. Front row: Roy Finch, who was transferred to Lincoln City in 1949; Harry Kinsell, a defensive strongman who played for England; goal-machine Dave Walsh; wing-wizard Billy Elliott, who scored 157 goals in 330 outings for the club between 1938 and 1951; Cyril Williams, secured from Bristol City and scorer of Albion's first Division One goal after the Second World War.

Action from the Albion *v.* Derby County First Division game at The Hawthorns in April 1950, which Albion won 1-0. Jimmy Dudley (on ground), Jack Vernon and Reg Ryan are the three Albion players while the lone Ram is Tim Ward.

Left: Goalkeeper Jimmy Sanders, born in London in 1920, spent thirteen years at The Hawthorns (1945 to 1958). Shot down by enemy aircraft during the war, he was understudy to Sam Bartram at Charlton Athletic before joining Albion. He went on to amass 391 appearances for the Baggies, gaining an FA Cup medal in 1954 after taking over from the injured Norman Heath a week or so before the final against Preston North End. A fine penalty-stopper, Sanders, who also helped Albion win promotion from the Second Division in 1948/49, moved to Coventry City from The Hawthorns and later became a publican. He now lives in Tamworth. *Right*: Glyn Hood made the first of his 74 appearances for Albion in an 8-1 home win over Chelsea in a Football League South match in 1945. A versatile half-back, he had joined the club two years earlier and remained at The Hawthorns until 1951, when he was forced to retire through injury. He now lives in Coventry.

54

While manfully helping Albion win promotion from the Second Division in 1948/49, inside forward Jack Haines was awarded his only England cap – and what an impact he made, scoring twice in a 6-0 win over Switzerland at Highbury halfway through that season. This is the first of Haines' two goals against the Swiss. He netted 23 times in 62 appearances for Albion before moving to Bradford.

In December 1950 Albion were beaten 3-1 in a local derby by Wolves at Molineux. Baggies goalkeeper Norman Heath is pictured twice punching clear from Wolves striker Roy Swinbourne.

Go for it – Albion players in pre-season training in readiness for the 1949/50 season. From left to right: Dave Walsh, Jack Vernon, Billy Elliott, Len Millard, Joe Kennedy, George Lee, Ray Barlow, Glyn Hood, Jack Haines, Jim Pemberton, Arthur Smith. Note the hooped shirts.

Shooting practice for Dave Walsh with Billy Elliott keeping an eye on proceedings.

Six
Goals Galore

Trainer and former centre forward W.G. Richardson (extreme right) puts the Albion players through a strenuous pre-season routine in July 1949 – getting them ready to tackle their first season back in the top flight since 1938. The players are, from left to right: Billy Brookes, Jack Haines, Jimmy Dudley, Billy Elliott, Gordon Inwood, Peter Hilton, Reg Ryan, Jim Pemberton, Jack Flavell, Dennis Gordon, Harry Homer, Eddie Wilcox, Glyn Hood, Arthur Smith.

Albion's second XI, pictured in September 1951, prior to their 3-0 defeat against Manchester United at Old Trafford. From left to right, back row: Hewson, Kennedy, Heath, Richardson, Hilton, Jenkins. Front row: Williams, Griffin, Horne, Carter, Cutler. Kennedy, Heath, Williams and Griffin all went on to give Albion excellent service, Kennedy and Griffin both gaining FA Cup winners' medals and Williams playing at full-back for Wales on 43 occasions – 33 during his time at the Hawthorns, thus making him Albion's most-capped player while serving with the club.

WEST BROMWICH ALBION		
	FOR	AGNS
1950		
Aug. 19—Aston Villa ....A		
„ 23—Newcastle Utd. ....A		
„ 26—Stoke City ....H		
„ 30—Newcastle Utd. ....H		
Sept. 2—Everton ....A		
„ 6—Middlesbrough ....A		
„ 9—Portsmouth ....H		
„ 13—Middlesbrough ....H		
„ 16—Chelsea ....A		
„ 23—Burnley ....H		
„ 30—Arsenal ....A		
Oct. 7—Derby County ....A		
„ 14—Liverpool ....H		
„ 18—Charlton Athletic ....A		
„ 21—Blackpool ....A		
„ 28—Tottenham H. ....H		
Nov. 4—Fulham ....A		
„ 11—Bolton W. ....H		
„ 25—(1) Manchester Utd. .....H		
Dec. 2—Wolverhamoton W. ......A		
„ 9—(2) Sunderland ....H		
„ 16—Aston Villa ....H		
„ 23—Stoke City ....A		
„ 25—Sheffield Wed. ....H		
„ 26—Sheffield Wed. ....A		
„ 30—Everton ....H		
·1951		
Jan 6—Third Round F.A. Cup		
„ 13—Portsmouth ....A		
„ 20—Chelsea ....H		
„ 27—Fourth Round F.A. Cup		
Feb. 3—Burnley ....A		
„ 10—Fifth Round F.A. Cup		
„ 17—Arsenal ....H		
„ 24—(6) Derby County ....H		
Mar. 3—Liverpool ....A		
„ 10—Blackpool ....H		
„ 17—Tottenham H. ....A		
„ 24—Fulham ....H		
„ 26—Huddersfield T. ....H		
„ 27—Huddersfield T. ....A		
„ 31—Bolton W. ....A		
April 7—Charlton Athletic ....H		
„ 14—Manchester Utd. ....A		
„ 21—Wolverhampton W. ....H		
„ 28—Sunderland ....A		
May 5—		

Left: Fixture card for 1950/51. *Right*: Dublin-born Reg Ryan, Albion's hard-tackling Irish international wing-half or inside forward, helped the club win promotion from the Second Division in 1949 and capture the FA Cup five years later. Paddy spent ten years at The Hawthorns (1945 to 1955) before moving to Derby County. A terrific competitor, he retired in 1960 with over 500 club and international games under his belt (432 for the Baggies). He died in Birmingham in 1997.

Albion on parade, September 1950. From left to right, back row: Jim Pemberton, Ron Floyd, Joe Kennedy, John McIlvenny, Grenville Jones, Mick Betteridge, Stan Rickaby, Norman Heath, Jimmy Dudley. Middle row: W.G. Richardson (trainer, standing), Ken Hodgkisson, Billy Owen, Allan Crowshaw, Jimmy Sanders, Glyn Hood, Dave Walsh, Jack Vernon, Tim Rawlings, Cyril Williams, Fred Richardson. Front row: Ray Barlow, Dennis Gordon, Billy Elliott, Ronnie Allen, Jack Smith (Albion's first official team manager), Arthur Smith, Len Millard, Peter Hill, Eddie Wilcox, Reg Ryan, Arthur Fitton (trainer).

This rare beermat is something of a collectors' item.

All dressed up and a game to play! Ronnie Allen, Len Millard, Andy McCall, Ray Barlow and Joe Kennedy pause for the camera as they arrive at Leeds Road, Huddersfield, for a First Division game against the Terriers in March 1951. A crowd of 32,401 saw the Baggies end a run of five matches without a win by beating the Yorkshire side 2-1, Ray Barlow netting both goals. Andy McCall had been signed from Blackpool two months earlier, having played for the Seasiders since 1947. He had a fine career as an inside forward, scoring 41 goals in 316 League appearances while also serving with Leeds United and Halifax Town. He had 32 outings for Albion, netting 3 goals. He was at Valley Parade on the day of the Bradford fire disaster on 11 May 1985, watching his son Stuart play for City against Lincoln, but thankfully he survived the tragedy.

George Lee (left) and Ronnie Allen – key members of Albion's forward line during the 1950s. Lee was a dashing left-winger, with pace and a powerful shot. Signed from Nottingham Forest for £12,000 in 1949, he scored 65 goals in 295 first-class games for the Baggies before quitting League soccer in 1958. An FA Cup winner in 1954, he later returned to the club as trainer/coach from 1959 to 1963, before taking over a similar position with Norwich City. He died in 1991, aged seventy-one. Allen cost Albion £20,000 when he transferred from Port Vale in March 1950. He was a brilliant footballer who occupied every front-line position for the Baggies, with centre forward undoubtedly being his best. He scored 234 goals for Albion in 415 appearances up to 1961 when he joined Crystal Palace. He was capped 5 times by England and scored twice in the 1954 FA Cup final win over Preston North End. Allen later became a successful manager, having two spells in charge at The Hawthorns as well as being boss of Wolves, Walsall, Athletic Bilbao, Sporting Lisbon and Panathinaikos. He played his last game of football for Albion in a friendly against Cheltenham Town in May 1995 at the age of sixty-six.

Albion's playing staff for the 1951/52 season. From left to right, back row: George Corbett, Peter Hilton, Mike Jenkins, Geoff Richards, Norman Heath, Jimmy Sanders, Reg Davies, Jimmy Dudley, George Lee, Fred Richardson, Arthur Smith. Middle row: Harry Ashley (trainer), Fred Pedley (physiotherapist), Arnold Charlesworth, Arthur Wright, Pat Hewson, Stuart Williams, Dennis Gordon, Stan Rickaby, Len Millard, Les Horne, Arthur Fitton (trainer), W.G. Richardson (coach/trainer). Front row: Frank Griffin, Wilf Carter, Jack Vernon, Ronnie Allen, Andy McCall.

Stan Rickaby (2) looks on as Baggies goalkeeper Jimmy Sanders safely gathers the ball during a League game at Old Trafford against Manchester United in December 1951. Unfortunately, Albion did not have the greatest of days out in Manchester, losing the game 5-1.

Jimmy Sanders collects a right-wing cross during Albion's 3-2 home League victory over Manchester City in November 1951. It was Sanders' first game back after injury. The three other players in close proximity are Dennis Westcott, the City centre forward (9), Stan Rickaby, Albion's right-back (2) and Jack Vernon keeping an eye on his 'keeper.

Goal for Ronnie Allen – the first for Albion in their 2-1 home win over Manchester City in February 1953. A crowd of almost 28,000 saw a tightly contested game and victory enabled the Baggies to complete the double over the Maine Road club, having won 1-0 earlier in the season. The German Bert Trautmann is the City goalkeeper and Frank Griffin looks on as full-back Roy Little makes a vain attempt to keep the ball out with his hand. Albion's other goal came from Ray Barlow.

Reg Ryan practises his shooting during a training session at The Hawthorns in January 1953. The goalkeeper is Norman Heath, the other two players are Ronnie Allen (left) and Johnny Nicholls, while trainer Arthur Fitton is ready to throw on the balls.

Watched by team-mate Jimmy Dudley (on his knee), Norman Heath, who contested the goalkeeping position with Sanders for nine years at the Hawthorns (1945 to 1954) comes to Albion's rescue during the First Division game against Arsenal at Highbury in March 1953. A crowd of over 50,000 saw the Baggies earn a point from a 0-0 draw.

In January 1953 Albion and Chelsea were involved in a long drawn-out fourth round FA Cup-tie. After four games and a total of more than 420 minutes of football, the Londoners finally won through with a 4-0 victory at Highbury. The initial clash ended 1-1 at Stamford Bridge; the replay finished 0-0 (after extra time) at The Hawthorns and the second replay at Villa Park was also squared up at 1-1 (again after extra time) before Chelsea romped home in the capital city, despite Norman Heath saving a penalty. *Above*: Goalmouth action inside the Albion penalty area as Chelsea press for the winner in the opening encounter at Stamford Bridge. *Below*: A pause in proceedings at Villa Park before the commencement of extra time in the third game. For the record, a total of over 158,400 spectators witnessed the four matches.

Season 1953/54 turned out to be Albion's best since 1930/31 and in some people's minds it was their best ever. The Baggies challenged Wolves all the way to the Football League Championship before having to settle for the runners-up spot but gained success in the FA Cup, winning the trophy for the fourth time by beating Preston North End 3-2 in the final at Wembley. En route to the Cup Final, Albion ousted Chelsea (1-0), Rotherham United (4-0), Newcastle United (3-2) and Tottenham Hotspur (3-0), all at The Hawthorns, and Port Vale (2-1) in the semi-final at Villa Park. *Top*: Left half Ray Barlow scored one of Albion's goals in their victory over Spurs – with this stunning twenty-five-yard free-kick. *Above*: Allen, with this winning penalty kick, was again on target in the semi-final against his former club Port Vale. *Right*: Ronnie Allen scored a hat-trick against Newcastle, depicted here by *Birmingham Evening Mail* cartoonist Norman Edwards.

Inspecting the Wembley turf. Albion players Frank Griffin, Stan Rickaby, Jimmy Dugdale, Ray Barlow, Jimmy Sanders (stooping), Jimmy Dudley and Johnny Nicholls with director Horace Thursfield (centre) out on the Wembley pitch on the Friday before the 1954 Cup Final.

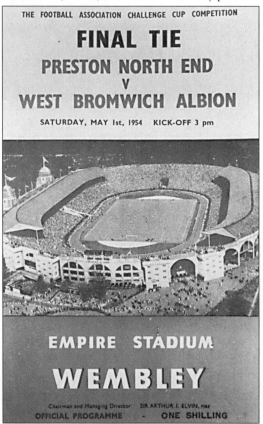

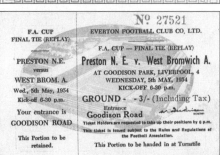

The programme cover and a ticket from the clash with Preston North End and also a ticket printed for the anticipated replay at Goodison Park.

The players take the field – Albion's left-back and skipper Len Millard (left) and Preston North End's England international right-winger Tom Finney lead out the two teams. Millard virtually marked Finney out of the game as Albion triumphed at Wembley for the second time in their history.

Almost 100,000 saw the 1954 FA Cup final. Ronnie Allen gave Albion a twenty-first minute lead, Angus Morrison equalised soon afterwards with a fine header and then early in the second half Charlie Wayman, looking yards offside, put North End 2-1 ahead. Albion weren't finished however and Ronnie Allen netted the equaliser from the penalty spot (after Tommy Docherty had brought down Ray Barlow) and Frank Griffin claimed a dramatic winner for Albion with just three minutes remaining. This photograph shows Griffin's delight as the ball goes past Preston 'keeper George Thompson.

Above: Cheers! Match-winner Frank Griffin celebrates his winning goal with a drop of bubbly from the trophy. Injured right-back Stan Rickaby looks on. *Below*: Over 150,000 supporters welcomed Albion back to West Bromwich as FA Cup winners in 1954.

Albion captain Len Millard giving a speech at a civic reception following the 1954 FA Cup final triumph.

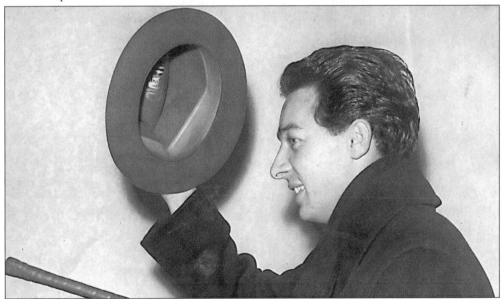

Ronnie Allen, Albion's two-goal hero in the 1954 FA Cup final, was a Frankie Vaughan fan and here he shows he can certainly do the business on the stage as well as on the soccer pitch! Allen spent eleven years at The Hawthorns (1950 to 1961). Signed from Port Vale for £20,000, he won 5 England caps and scored 234 goals in 415 senior games for the Baggies. The complete footballer, he later had two spells as manager at the club and was also in charge of neighbours Walsall and Wolves, as well as managing and coaching several foreign clubs.

Albion manager Vic Buckingham, appointed in 1953, inspects The Hawthorns pitch as club physiotherapist Fred Pedley looks on.

An Albion board meeting in progress at The Hawthorns during the 1953/54 season with chairman H. Wilson Keys conducting the proceedings. Manager Vic Buckingham is seated second left with Tommy Glidden to his left. Secretary Eph Smith is on the chairman's right.

Albion and Wolverhampton Wanderers were involved in a terrific battle for the League Championship in 1953/54. At the end of the day, Wolves took the star prize by just four points (managing 57 to Albion's 53). They completed the double over Albion during the season, winning both games 1-0. The photograph here shows Wolves and England goalkeeper Bert Williams saving a close range shot from Albion left-winger George Lee (grounded on right) with Bill Shorthouse challenging. Frank Griffin and Ronnie Allen are the other Albion players.

Ronnie Allen was also a fine golfer and here he drives off the fifth tee at the Sandwell golf course with his manager Vic Buckingham looking on. Allen won the Professional Footballers' golf championship in 1959 and 1961 and finished runner-up in 1963 and 1964.

Four months after beating Preston in the 1954 FA Cup final, Albion met the Deepdale club in a League game at The Hawthorns and this time gained two First Division points with a 2-0 victory. The picture here shows Frank Griffin and Wilf Carter looking on as Ronnie Allen's twenty-five-yard rocket whistles past goalkeeper George Thompson for Albion's second goal. The attendance was 41,125.

Johnny Nicholls (padded up) and Ronnie Allen (acting as umpire) both loved scoring goals – and their cricket. They were known as the 'terrible twins' and between them netted almost 300 goals for the Baggies. They played for England in two internationals together and in 1953/54, when Albion came so near to completing the League and FA Cup double, they weighed in with a staggering 66 goals – 55 of them in the First Division – with Allen notching 34 and Nicholls 32.

Since the early 1950s, games between Albion and Manchester United have invariably been cracking affairs with plenty of goals for the spectators to cheer. In the pre-Munich years Albion perhaps had the better of the exchanges against the Old Trafford club and in November 1954 a crowd of 33,267 saw the Baggies win a First Division encounter at The Hawthorns 2-0 with goals by Johnny Nicholls and Ronnie Allen. Here, Wilf Carter (stripes) and United's Roger Byrne look on as Nicholls' drive finds the net for Albion's opener.

Wilf Carter, a local-born utility forward from Wednesbury, who acted as reserve for both Ronnie Allen and Johnny Nicholls on numerous occasions, is seen here getting in a shot against Arsenal at Highbury in December 1955. The Gunners' challenge is coming in from Cliff Holton.

Ray Barlow, pictured in action against Arsenal at Highbury, served Albion for sixteen years (1944 to 1960). Spotted by former Albion centre forward Jimmy Cookson playing in Swindon works football, he developed into a brilliant player, occupying the centre half, left half, centre forward and inside left positions for the Baggies. However, it was as a left half that he shone most of all, helping Albion win the FA Cup in 1954, having earlier assisted them in gaining promotion from the Second Division in 1949. He won just a single England cap (goodness knows why) and appeared in 482 games, scoring 48 goals for Albion, before moving to Birmingham City. Born in Swindon in 1926, Ray now lives in Pedmore.

Goalkeeper Jimmy Sanders cuts out a dangerous right-wing cross during Albion's home League game against Arsenal in December 1956. The Gunners' player in the foreground is Derek Tapscott with Joe Kennedy behind him and Don Howe ready to clear if his 'keeper slips up. Albion lost the game 2-0.

Ray Barlow, Joe Kennedy and Jimmy Dudley formed a brilliant half-back line for the Albion during the 1950s. Between them the trio amassed some 1,200 appearances and 63 goals for the club. All three were of international class, but only Barlow represented his country at senior level. Kennedy (England) and Dudley (Scotland) both appeared in 'B' internationals. Kennedy spent thirteen years at The Hawthorns (1948 to 1961) and Dudley fifteen (1944 to 1959). What would this trio fetch on the transfer market today?

The same can be said about Derek Kevan, who joined Albion in 1953 from Bradford Park Avenue. He developed into a magnificent goalscoring centre forward, as strong as an ox, fearless and totally committed. Known as 'The Tank', he served the Baggies for ten years during which time he scored 173 goals in 291 first team appearances, lining up alongside the likes of Ronnie Allen, Bobby Robson, Brian Whitehouse, Keith Smith and Davey Burnside among others. He netted 8 times in his 14 international appearances for England and during a fine career also served with Chelsea, Manchester City, Luton Town, Crystal Palace, Peterborough United and Stockport.

In 1956/57 Albion almost made it to Wembley for the second time in three years – but on this occasion they lost their FA Cup semi-final 1-0 to neighbours Aston Villa in a replay at St Andrew's after playing out a 2-2 draw at Molineux. *Above*: In the quarter-final replay at Arsenal Brian Whitehouse scored what looked like an 'offside' goal which took Albion through to meet the Villa. *Below*: Whitehouse found the net in the Villa game, scoring twice in the clash at Molineux. This photograph shows one of his efforts flying past 'keeper Nigel Sims.

More action from Albion's sixth
round replay with Arsenal in 1957
with goalkeeper Jimmy Sanders
punching clear as Don Howe (2)
and Ray Barlow look on.

Villa goalkeeper
Nigel Sims
clears his lines
during the 1957
semi-final replay
at St Andrew's.
Brian
Whitehouse is
the Albion
player with Pat
Saward in close
attention.

The two FA Cup semi-final matches in 1957 featured three Midland clubs – Aston Villa, Birmingham City and West Bromwich Albion. Before the scheduled matches (Villa *v.* Albion and City *v.* Manchester United) a special photograph was taken featuring all the players from the three Midland clubs with the respestive managers, trainers and coaches. From left to right, back row: R. Graham (WBA trainer), J. Sanders, D. Pace, J. Dugdale, W. Moore (AV trainer), P. Saward, G. Merrick, R. Shaw (BC coach). Fourth row: F. Griffin, D. Howe, W. Myerscough, J. Sewell, T. Birch, P. McParland, K.O. Roberts, B. Orritt, J. Newman, G. Clark (WBA assistant trainer). Third row: A. Turner (BC manager), J. Kennedy, L. Millard, J. Dudley, P. Aldis, S. Lynn, N. Sims, G. Astall, J. Watts, P. Murphy, V. Buckingham (WBA manager). Second row: E. Houghton (AV manager), R. Horobin, M. Setters, R. Allen, W. Baxter, S. Crowther, L. Smith, N. Kinsey, T. Smith, K. Green. Front row: R. Robson, B. Whitehouse, D. Kevan, R. Barlow, J. Dixon, R. Warhurst, E. Brown, J. Hall, A. Govan.

Here are the three team captains – from left to right: Roy Warhurst of Birmingham City, Albion's Ray Barlow and Johnny Dixon of Aston Villa – shaking hands before the matches took place.

At the end of the 1956/57 season, Albion were invited to tour USSR. They played three games behind the Iron Curtain, winning two and drawing the other, thus becoming the first club to win in the USSR. Here, the Albion players pose for the camera in Moscow's Red Square. From left to right, back row: Frank Griffin, Jimmy Sanders, Don Howe, Joe Kennedy, Stuart Williams, Ronnie Allen, Fred Brown, Len Millard, Derek Kevan, Ray Barlow. Front row: George Lee, Bobby Robson, Brian Whitehouse, Maurice Setters, Roy Horobin, Jimmy Dudley.

Here we see Jimmy Dudley, Ronnie Allen and Ray Barlow with an ardent Albion supporter who made his way over to Russia. For the record, Albion's two victories in the USSR were 3-0 against Dynamo Tbilisi and 4-2 over the CDSA (Russian Army side) while they shared the spoils with FC Zenit at 1-1. In October 1957 the Army side came over to England for a friendly to officially switch on the The Hawthorns floodlights. A crowd of 52,805 saw Albion win a thrilling contest 6-5.

Albion manager Vic Buckingham (second left) with skipper Ray Barlow and players Jimmy Dudley and Frank Griffin pose for the camera whilst on tour in Russia in 1957.

Derek Kevan accepts a tankard after being voted West Bromwich Albion supporters' Player of the Year in 1957. Ronnie Allen is seen bottom left with former Supporters' Club chairman 'Dave' Welsh above him.

Davey Burnside was a brilliant ball juggler and not a bad inside forward either. He spent eight years at The Hawthorns (1955 to 1963) during which time he scored 42 goals in 135 games. He later played for Southampton, Crystal Palace, Plymouth Argyle, Wolves, Colchester United and Bristol City. He became a qualified FA Coach and was England's youth team manager in the 1980s.

Left: In 1958 Albion met Manchester United in a sixth round FA Cup-tie soon after the tragic Munich air crash. A crowd of over 58,000 packed into The Hawthorns to see the tie and with time fast running out and United leading 2-1, Roy Horobin scored a dramatic late equaliser for the Baggies. United's 'keeper Harry Gregg claimed the ball never crossed the line, but this picture clearly shows it did! Albion lost the replay 1-0 inside a packed and emotional Old Trafford, but then a few days later they went back and hammered United 4-0 on the same ground in a League game … funny old game football! *Right*: Goalkeeper Fred Brown, seen here during a pre-season practice game at The Hawthorns, was signed from Aldershot in 1955 as cover for Jimmy Sanders. He failed to live up to expectations and made only 11 first team appearances before leaving the club in 1958.

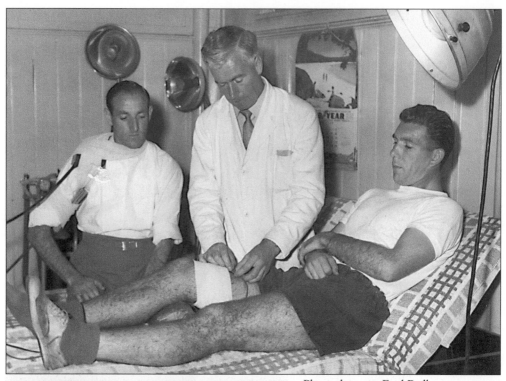

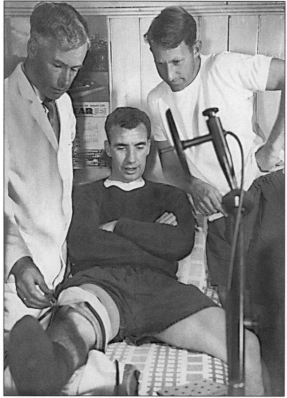

Physiotherapist Fred Pedley spent fifteen years at The Hawthorns (1950 to 1965) and here he checks out a knee injury suffered by Stuart Williams, Albion's Welsh international full-back. Derek Hogg is the player waiting to jump onto the couch. Williams spent twelve years at the club (1950 to 1962) and played alongside his namesake Graham for both Albion and Wales. Flying left-winger Hogg joined Albion from Leicester City in 1958 and left for Cardiff City in 1961.

Frank Griffin, the 1954 FA Cup hero, also receives treatment for a knee injury. Ray Barlow is an interested onlooker. Griffin's Albion career was virtually ended when he broke his leg in an FA Cup replay against Sheffield United in February 1958. He joined the club in 1951 and left for Northampton Town in 1959 after scoring 52 goals in 275 appeareances for the Baggies. Griffin was, of course, the man who netted that dramatic winner at Wembley in 1954.

Pre-season training with the ball at The Hawthorns in 1958. Left to right: goalkeeper Clive Jackman, right-winger Jimmy Campbell, wing half Maurice Setters, skipper Ray Barlow, right-back Don Howe, Welsh international Stuart Williams, outside left Roy Horobin, wing half Chuck Drury, strikers Ronnie Allen and Derek Kevan, centre half Joe Kennedy.

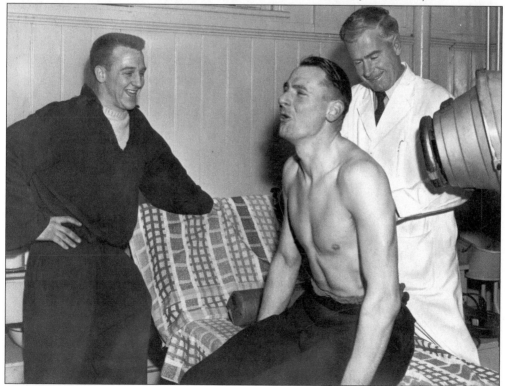

Maurice Setters, who later played for Manchester United, Stoke City, Charlton Athletic and Coventry City, made 132 appearances for Albion during his five years with the club (1955 to 1960). Here, he enjoys a laugh as first team trainer Dick Graham gets some hot treatment from physiotherapist Fred Pedley.

In October 1958, Albion put on a superb performance to beat Aston Villa 4-1 in a League match at Villa Park. Here, home 'keeper Nigel Sims foils Davey Burnside as the Baggies press towards the Witton End. A crowd of 47,124 saw Burnside, Derek Hogg, Don Howe (penalty) and Bobby Robson score for Albion after Villa had taken the lead through Ken Barrett.

Albion were a great cup team in the 1950s and '60s. In the fourth round of the 1959 FA Cup they defeated Brentford 2-0 at home in front of almost 42,000 fans. Here, Gerry Cakebread, the Bees 'keeper, dives to cut out a right-wing centre aimed for Derek Kevan (dark shirt). Unfortunately, Albion went out to Blackpool 3-1 in the next round of the competition.

Seven
Cup Glory and Europe

Albion line up for the camera at the start of the 1963/64 season, just prior to their first home game against Leicester City which ended 1-1. From left to right, back row: Kenny Foggo, Terry Simpson, Stan Jones, Ray Potter, Bobby Cram, Graham Williams. Front row: John Kaye, Ronnie Fenton, Don Howe (captain) Clive Clark, Bobby Hope. The mascot is Dave Winwood.

Left: Wolverhampton-born right-back Don Howe won 23 England caps and appeared in 379 first-class games for Albion from 1955 to 1964, later returning to The Hawthorns as manager from 1971 to 1975. He left Albion for Arsenal and later coached and/or managed a number of top sides. He has also been a key figure in coaching the full England side and the under-21s. *Right*: Bobby Robson, seen here in action against Sunderland in 1958, joined Albion two years earlier from Fulham for £25,000. He returned to the London club in 1962 for £20,000 after scoring 61 goals in 257 appearances for the Baggies as well as winning 20 England caps. He later managed Fulham, Ipswich Town, England (1982 to 1990), PSV Eindhoven, Sporting Lisbon, Barcelona, FC Porto and Newcastle United.

Left: Speedy outside left Clive Clark was a £17,000 buy from QPR in 1961. He became a star performer in Albion's first team, scoring 98 goals in 353 outings before returning to Loftus Road in 1969. Capped by England at under-23 level, Clark scored the first ever League Cup goal at Wembley (in 1967) and helped Albion win both the League Cup (1966) and FA Cup (1968). *Right*: Full-backs Stuart Williams (left) and Graham Williams won 70 Welsh caps between them, with Stuart gaining a club record 33 with Albion (44 in total). They also amassed a total of 606 first team appearances for the Baggies – Stuart 246 from 1952 to 1962 and Graham 360 from 1955 to 1972. Stuart also played for Wrexham and Southampton and later became Albion's trainer, while Graham skippered Albion to victory in both the 1966 League Cup and 1968 FA Cup finals. He later became a successful coach, mainly working abroad. He was in charge of Cardiff City (during 1981/82) and was also the Welsh national team's assistant-manager under former Albion centre forward and manager Bobby Gould.

Gordon Clark, the former Manchester City full-back and chief scout at The Hawthorns, was appointed manager in 1959 in succession to Vic Buckingham. He was to leave the club a third of the way through the 1961/62 season, three months after this team photograph was taken. From left to right, back row: Jack Lovatt, Peter Billingham, Stan Jones, Ray Potter, Wilf Dixon (trainer), Jock Wallace, Derek Kevan, Stuart Williams, Bobby Cram. Middle row: Clive Clark, Graham Williams, Chuck Drury, Bobby Robson, Gordon Clark, Don Howe, Alec Jackson, Davey Burnside. Front row: Keith Smith, Geoff Carter, Bobby Hope, Colin Brookes, Jackie Bannister, Brian Macready.

Left: Centre forward Jack 'Shack' Lovatt played in 18 League games for Albion and scored 5 goals. It was hoped he would take over from Ronnie Allen but he never quite fitted the bill and left The Hawthorns in 1963 for Nuneaton Borough. *Right*: Goalkeeper Ray Potter, seen here during a League game at West Ham, joined Albion from Crystal Palace in 1958. Over the next nine years he made 238 first-team appearances before losing his place to John Osborne. He won a League Cup winners' prize in 1966.

Left: Bobby Cram, seen in action during Albion's 6-1 defeat at the hands of West Ham in 1965 (England striker Geoff Hurst is the Hammers' player in shot), appeared in 163 games between 1959 and 1967, scoring 26 goals, most of them penalties. Usually a right-back, he netted a hat-trick from that position against Stoke City in 1964, becoming only the second defender to achieve that feat in the top division. He is the uncle of athlete Steve Cram. *Right*: Outside right Kenny Foggo, a Scotsman born in Perth in 1943, made his League debut in 1962 and went on to score 29 goals in 136 outings before moving to Norwich City in 1967. He later played for Portsmouth, Brentford and Southend United.

Tipton-born utility forward Alec Jackson (on the ball during a practice session in 1964), spent ten years at The Hawthorns during which he netted 52 goals in 208 matches. A tremendous ball player, he enjoyed more success on the right-wing than anywhere else and made a scoring debut against Charlton in 1954 at the age of seventeen. The other players are Don Howe and Kenny Foggo (right).

Albion drew 3-3 at home with Arsenal in a fourth round FA Cup-tie in January 1964, Stan Jones scoring a rare goal in front of almost 40,000 fans. The replay at Highbury attracted a crowd of 57,698, but despite a plucky performance by the Baggies they went out of the competition, beaten 2-0. Here, the Albion defence (with Don Howe, right, and Stan Jones, centre, prominent) contest an Arsenal corner in the first half.

Albion's senior, reserve and intermediate players along with the management and coaching staff at the 1964 pre-season photocall at The Hawthorns. Seated on the ground on the extreme left of the photograph is Tony Brown, who was to become Albion's greatest ever goalscorer and appearance-maker. He served the club for twenty years from 1961 to 1981.

Albion were always a match for Liverpool in the 1960s and this picture shows an aerial dual at Anfield involving Albion defender Stan Jones and striker John Kaye (9) and Liverpool's centre half Ron Yeats in 1966. The game ended in a 2-2 draw.

This is Albion's League Cup-winning squad. From left to right, back row: G. Lovett, S. Jones, B. Hope, J. Astle, D. Fraser. Middle row: G. Williams, G. Howshall, R. Fairfax, R. Potter, D. Campbell, B. Cram. Front row: J. Hagan, T. Brown, I. Collard, J. Kaye, C. Clark, A. McPherson (trainer).

Left: John Osborne, seen here collecting a high ball during a game against Nottingham Forest, joined Albion from Chesterfield in 1967. Over the next eleven years he made 312 appearances for the Baggies, gaining an FA Cup winners' medal in 1968. One of the club's greatest goalkeepers, Ossie died of cancer in 1998. *Right*: Tough-tacking defender Doug Fraser was a bargain £25,000 buy from Aberdeen in 1963. He spent eight years at The Hawthorns, starring in 325 games (12 goals scored). He played in three League Cup finals (1966, 1967, 1970), skippering the side in the latter. He won an FA Cup winners' medal in 1968, gained 2 caps for Scotland and after leaving Albion played for Nottingham Forest and Walsall, later becoming manager of the Saddlers.

Left: John Kaye joined Albion as a striker from Scunthorpe United, but left after establishing himself as a superb defender. Between 1963 and 1971 he appeared in 361 games for Albion (54 goals scored), gaining both League Cup and FA Cup winner's prizes. He was a thoroughbred professional and a terrific club man. He played for and later managed Hull City after leaving The Hawthorns. *Right*: Jeff Astle – the 'King' – scored 168 goals in 361 appearances for Albion between 1964 and 1974. A huge favourite with the fans, he was the First Division's top marksman in 1969/70 with 25 goals and in 1968 scored in every round of the FA Cup, his extra-time winner at Wembley against Everton bringing the Baggies their fifth triumph in the competition. He netted six hat-tricks for the club, including two in a week in September 1965 and two in seventy-two hours in April 1968! This picture shows Astle with junior supporters in 1968.

Above: Gerry Howshall (4) scores a spectacular goal for Albion in their 2-2 draw with Chelsea at Stamford Bridge in April 1965. Twenty-four hours earlier Albion had crashed 6-1 at West Ham when Brian Dear scored five goals in double-quick time. *Below*: Albion players wait to board the team coach for an away game in 1966. Long-serving club secretary Alan Everiss, who later became a director, is standing on the extreme left of the picture while (Sir) Bert Millichip is on the right of the group.

In 1967 Albion went back to Wembley for the first time in thirteen years when they met Third Division champions-elect Queens Park Rangers in the League Cup final. As holders of the trophy the Baggies were expected to win and looked odds-on favourites at half-time when holding a two-goal lead, both scored by former Rangers star Clive Clark. However, a tactical switch back-fired in the second half and Rangers stormed back to win 3-2 in front of almost 98,000 fans. Here, the two teams walk out before the 3.30 p.m. kick-off on 4 March 1967.

Dick Sheppard, seen here diving in the Highbury mud to prevent future Baggies centre forward Bobby Gould from getting to the ball, was reserve goalkeeper to John Osborne for a number of years at The Hawthorns. He played in 54 games for the club, including the 1967 League Cup final, before transferring to Bristol Rovers in 1969. Sheppard died in 1998 of a heart attack.

In 1968 Albion reached their third major final in as many years, this time the FA Cup. Having knocked out Colchester United, Southampton, Portsmouth and Liverpool (the latter at the third attempt), the Baggies entered the semi-final where they met Birmingham City. Jeff Astle and Tony Brown scored a goal apiece to see off the Blues at Villa Park and then at Wembley it was Astle's extra-time winner that beat Everton 1-0 to bring Albion their fifth triumph in the competition. *Above*: 'Bomber' Brown drives home his semi-final goal against Blues at Villa Park. *Below*: Jeff Astle cracks his left-footed winner past Everton's goalkeeper Gordon West in the final.

Skipper Graham Williams holds aloft the FA Cup after Albion's success over Everton in the 1968 Cup Final. Also in the picture are, from left to right: centre half John Talbut, signed from Burnley to replace Stan Jones; Clive Clark, with the trophy lid; scoring hero Jeff Astle; Doug Fraser; Dennis Clarke, the first substitute ever used at Wembley when he came on for the injured John Kaye at the end of normal time; Kaye himself (with plinth); Bobby Hope.

As in 1954, thousands of supporters welcomed the Albion players back to West Bromwich in 1968. Reports say that upwards of 250,000 people lined the route from New Street station in Birmingham to the town hall in West Bromwich – a distance of some five and a half miles.

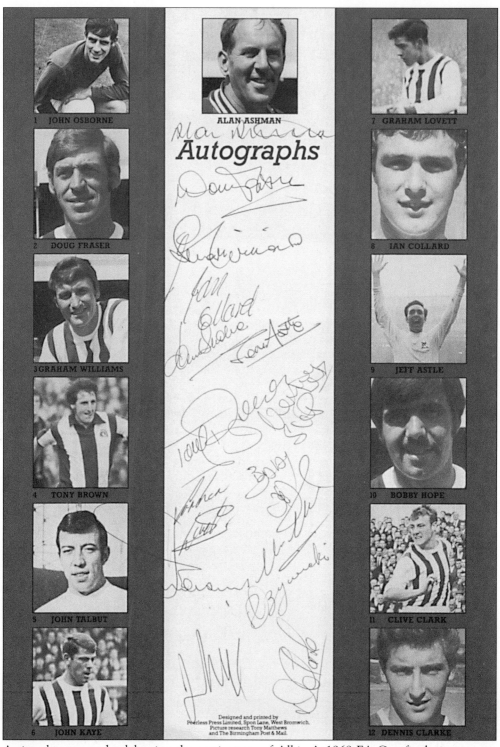

A signed menu card celebrating the anniversary of Albion's 1968 FA Cup final victory over Everton.

Albion began the 1968/69 season with a home game against Sheffield Wednesday. This was the twelve-man squad that drew 0-0 with the Owls. From left to right, back row: Alan Merrick, Bobby Hope, Jeff Astle, Tony Brown, Dick Krzywicki, Dick Sheppard, John Talbut. Front row: Ronnie Rees (Welsh international winger signed from Coventry City), Doug Fraser, John Kaye, Graham Williams, Asa Hartford.

As holders of the FA Cup, Albion qualified to take part in the European Cup Winners' Cup competition. They reached the quarter-final stage after knocking out the Belgium side RFC Brugge and Dimamo Bucharest, each over two legs. This picture shows Asa Hartford scoring Albion's goal in the 1-1 draw in Bucharest. The second leg ended in a 4-0 win. However, after holding the Scottish Cup winners Dunfermline Athletic to a goalless draw in the away leg, the Baggies failed to do the business on a freezing cold night at The Hawthorns and lost the next round 1-0 on aggregate. Midfielder Hartford had joined Albion in 1966, turned professional on his seventeenth birthday and went on to score 26 goals in 275 games for the club before moving to Manchester City for £225,000 in 1974. He won 50 caps for Scotland during his career and amassed well over 800 appearances at club level while also serving with Everton, Nottingham Forest, Bolton Wanderers, Norwich City, Stockport County, Oldham Athletic and Shrewsbury Town.

Left: Inside forward Colin Suggett, seen here in action against West Ham, was Albion's first six-figure signing, joining the club from Sunderland in 1969 for £100,000. He went on to score 30 goals in 170 appearances before transferring to Norwich City in 1973. *Right*: Alan Ashman, a former Nottingham Forest centre forward, was Albion's manager from 1967 to 1971. During that time the team won the FA Cup, were runners-up in the League Cup, reached the quarter-finals of the European Cup Winners' Cup and finished as high as eighth in the First Division. Ashman had succeeded Jimmy Hagan and was replaced by ex-player Don Howe.

Albion's 1969/70 senior squad. Left to right, back row: Dick Krzywicki, Lyndon Hughes, Dennis Martin, Jeff Astle, John Osborne, John Talbut, John Kaye, Graham Williams, Jimmy Dunn (trainer). Front row: Asa Hartford, Tony Brown, Ray Wilson, Alan Ashman, Doug Fraser, Colin Suggett, Bobby Hope.

Arms up … legs apart … jump – Doug Fraser in the Albion gymnasium watched by, from left to right: Dennis Martin, John Talbut, Jim Cumbes, Tony Brown (behind him), Ray Wilson, John Kaye, Bobby Hope, Asa Hartford.

Albion players relax as they join in a sing-song with local TV and radio personality Mr Joe 'Piano' Henderson in 1969. The players are, from left to right: John Talbut, Colin Suggett, Graham Williams, Stuart Williams (trainer, behind him), Tony Brown, manager Alan Ashman, John Kaye with Doug Fraser (behind him), Pete Freeman (in front of Danny Hegan), Jim Cumbes, Asa Hartford, Dick Krzywicki, Bobby Hope.

Colin Suggett (8), challenged by Jackie Marsh, still manages to get in a shot on the Stoke City goal during a League game at The Victoria ground in January 1971. The Stoke 'keeper is of course England star Gordon Banks.

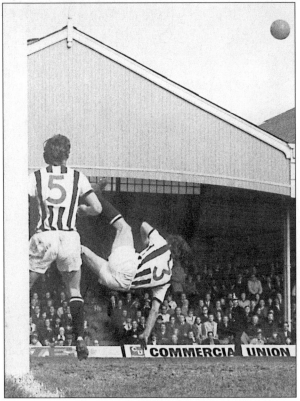

Albion's centre half and skipper John Wile (5) watches his colleague and left-back Ray Wilson (3) acrobatically clear the danger during a First Division game against arch rivals Wolverhampton Wanderers at Molineux in April 1972. Albion won the game 1-0 with a Tony Brown goal.

Eight

Mixed Fortunes

The goal that sent 15,000 Albion supporters into a frenzy! It was the one Tony Brown scored at Boundary Park in April 1976 that earned Albion a 1-0 victory over Oldham Athletic and ensured their return to the First Division under player-manager Johnny Giles.

Centre half John Wile, now chief executive at The Hawthorns, was an Albion player from December 1970 until June 1983. During that time he made exactly 500 League appearances and starred in 619 first team games overall and more than 700 including friendlies. He was twenty-three when he moved to The Hawthorns for £30,000 from Peterborough United – a terrific signing by manager Alan Ashman. He became team captain and was one of the best uncapped central defenders in the country during the period 1976 to 1980, when he formed a tremendous partnership with Ally Robertson at the heart of the Baggies' defence. He played more matches at centre half than any other Albion player and his courageous performance in the 1978 FA Cup semi-final against Ipswich will never be forgotten. It was a pity he never played at Wembley, although he did have the honour of helping the Baggies win promotion to the First Division in 1976. The three pictures on this page show John being nice to an opponent at The Hawthorns (above left), with pop star and Baggies fan Eric Clapton (above right) and in action against Nottingham Forest (left).

Willie Johnston was a record £138,000 signing by Albion boss Don Howe from Glasgow Rangers in December 1972. A flying left-winger with great on-the-ball ability, Johnston also had a fiery temper and was sent-off nineteen times during an eventful career – as well as being flown back home from the 1978 World Cup finals in Argentina. He won 22 caps for Scotland (13 with Albion) and during his six and a quarter years at The Hawthorns scored 28 goals in 261 first-class matches, creating many more openings for the likes of Tony and Ally Brown, Cyrille Regis and Laurie Cuningham. Johnston played for Vancouver Whitecaps, Birmingham City, Rangers (again) and Hearts after leaving Albion, before becoming a coach and then a licensee in Kirkcaldy.

This picture, taken on 21 October 1972, captures the moment when Bobby Gould (not in picture) scored Albion's goal in their 1-0 victory over his former club Wolverhampton Wanderers at The Hawthorns. The Albion player ready to celebrate is young substitute Stewart Woolgar who was appearing in only his second League game.

In January 1974 Second Division Albion were drawn away to First Division Everton in the fourth round of the FA Cup. The tie was played on a Sunday and in front of 53,509 fans the Baggies gained a creditable 0-0 draw. They went on to win the replay 1-0 before losing to the eventual runners-up Newcastle United in the next round. This picture shows Albion's Asa Hartford getting in a shot during the game at Everton despite the attentions of Mickey Bernard.

Dave Rusbury and Len Cantello challenge Frank Carrodus, the Aston Villa midfielder, during a local derby at Villa Park in March 1975. Over 47,500 fans saw Albion lose the Second Division game 3-1.

In the summer of 1975, after two years of Second Division football, Albion appointed their first-ever player-manager when Johnny Giles arrived from Leeds United. The former Manchester United winger and Republic of Ireland international transformed Albion from a mediocre side into one good enough and strong enough to play in Europe. He signed some terrific players – Laurie Cunningham, Mick Martin and Paddy Mulligan to name just three. He got the team working like a machine and at the end of his first season became a hero, worshipped by thousands, as Albion won 1-0 at Oldham to clinch promotion. He left The Hawthorns after two seasons only to return in the mid-1980s when Albion were again struggling. However, on this occasion he couldn't turn things round. But what a player and what a manager – one of the finest Albion have ever signed for just £48,000.

Jubilant Albion supporters – some of the 15,000 who travelled to Oldham – join Johnny Giles, Paddy Mulligan and goalkeeper John Osborne in the director's box at Boundary Park on 25 April 1976 to celebrate promotion.

Laurie Cunningham (left) and Cyrille Regis. Cunningham cost £110,000 from Leyton Orient in March 1977 and scored 30 goals in 114 games before moving to Real Madrid for nearly £1 million in 1979. An England international, he later played for Manchester United and gained an FA Cup winners' medal with Wimbledon in 1988. Sadly, Laurie died in a car crash on the outskirts of Madrid in July 1989, aged thirty-three. Regis, a bargain £5,000 capture from non-League Hayes in 1977 became a cult hero at The Hawthorns. He served Albion for seven years, scoring 112 goals in 302 senior appearances before transferring to Coventry City. Like his buddy Cunningham, Regis won an FA Cup winners' medal after leaving – with the Sky Blues in 1987. Regis also played for England, Aston Villa and Wolves. In the late 1990s he returned to Albion as coach, but left in March 2000.

Left: Ron Atkinson did a great job during his first spell as manager from 1978 to 1981, guiding Albion to the quarter-finals of the 1979 UEFA Cup and the FA Cup semi-finals. He got the team playing magnificent, attacking football before he left for Manchester United. Unfortunately, soon after leaving he took both Bryan Robson and Remi Moses away from The Hawthorns – and was never forgiven for doing that. Atkinson, like Johnny Giles and Ronnie Allen, returned for a second spell in charge of Albion but did not get it right again. Atkinson, a player with Oxford United, also managed a number of clubs. *Right*: Bryan Robson played in 249 games and scored 46 goals for Albion before leaving The Hawthorns to join Manchester United for a record £1.5 million in October 1981. Robson won honours galore at Old Trafford and took his tally of England caps up to 90 before moving to Middlesbrough in 1994. He appeared in almost 500 competitive matches for United, gaining numerous domestic and European honours.

In the UEFA Cup competition of 1978/79, Albion beat Galatasary (Turkey), Sporting Braga (Portugal) and Valencia (Spain) before losing in the quarter-finals to Red Star Belgrade (Yugoslavia). This picture shows Man of the Match Laurie Cunningham scoring Albion's goal in the away leg against Valencia which ended in a 1-1 draw.

This team group was taken prior to kick-off against Red Star Belgrade in Yugoslavia. The players are, from left to right, back row: Brendon Batson, Ally Robertson, Tony Godden, Cyrille Regis, Bryan Robson, Ally Brown. Front row: Derek Statham, Tony Brown, John Wile, Laurie Cunningham, John Trewick. A crowd of over 95,000 saw the Baggies lose the game 1-0. They went on to draw the home leg 1-1 and go our of the competition.

**BRITISH FOOTBALL
TOUR TO CHINA
MAY 1978**

"Friendship first, competition second"

WEST BROMWICH ALBION

TOUR ARRANGED JOINTLY BY
THE FOOTBALL ASSOCIATION AND
LONDON EXPORT CORPORATION

OFFICIAL TOUR PROGRAMME

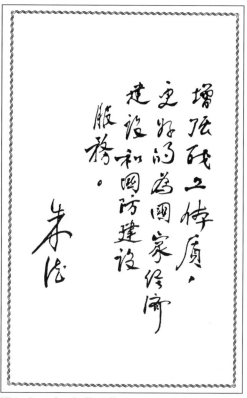

In May 1979, following a splendid season of UEFA Cup football, Albion visited the People's Republic of China. Here they played four games, won them all, made thousands of friends and on the return journey stopped off and won a fifth match in Hong Kong. John Wile proved to be a marvellous ambassador and John Trewick's comments on the Great Wall of China were heard in Australia! *Below*: Director Tom Silk (left) and chairman Bert Millichip walk round the perimeter of the pitch before the start of Albion's game against a Shanghai XI, which they won 2-0.

Nine

The Dismal
Eighties

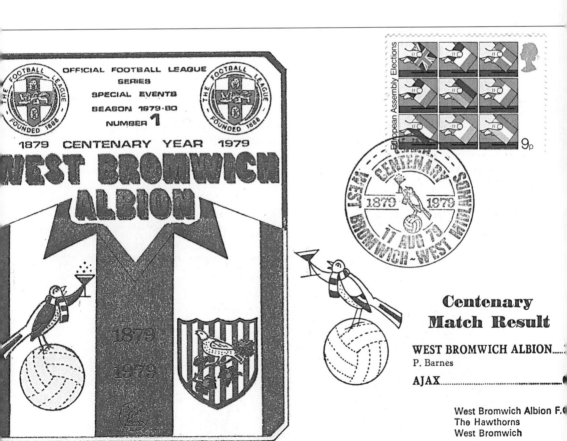

A first day cover to celebrate 100 years of West Bromwich Albion FC.

Albion officially celebrated their centenary in 1979 and in the same year several new players arrived. *Above*: From left to right: Derek Statham, Bryan Robson, Peter Barnes, Gary Owen, John Deehan. Statham had a fine career with Albion, appearing in 378 games from 1976 to 1987 before moving to Southampton for £100,000. One of the best attacking left-backs in the country, he was unfortunate to win only 3 England caps. Left-winger Barnes, fast and clever with an excellent shot, was signed from Manchester City in July 1979 for £748,000. He was a match-winner on his day and netted 25 goals in 92 games before moving to Leeds for £930,000 in 1981. Owen also came from Manchester City for £465,000, two months before Barnes. A skilful midfielder, he spent seven seasons, making 229 first team appearances with 29 goals. Owen also won 22 caps for England's under-21 side. Deehan was considered the ideal striker to partner Cyrille Regis and cost £424,000 from Aston Villa. Unfortunately, he never settled and after netting just 5 goals in 50 games he was sold to Norwich City for £175,000. *Below left*: In January 1979 inside forward David Mills became the costliest footballer in Great Britain when Ron Atkinson paid £518,000 to Middlesbrough. Mills, whom it was hoped would replace Tony Brown, never really fitted in and after scoring 6 goals in 76 appearances he was transferred to Sheffield Wednesday for £30,000. *Below right*: Irish international midfielder Mick Martin (left) and Scottish-born defender Ally Robertson were key figures in the 1970s side. Martin, signed by Johnny Giles from Manchester United, won 52 caps for the Republic of Ireland and played 115 games for Albion. Robertson joined Albion as a teenager in 1968 and stayed at The Hawthorns until 1986. He made 626 appearances for Albion, more than 570 of them as John Wile's partner. He had a record run of 171 consecutive League games, beating Jimmy Dudley's previous tally of 166.

Tony Brown spent twenty years as a player at The Hawthorns (1961 to 1981). During that time 'Bomber' created records galore: most competitive goals for Albion (279, 218 of them in the League), most senior appearances (720), most League outings (574) and most penalties scored (over 50). Born in Oldham in 1945, he played mainly as an attacking midfielder, occupying the right half berth, although he did fill all five forward-line positions during his time with the Baggies. He formed a fine partnership with Jeff Astle and then Cyrille Regis, but for all his efforts gained just a single England cap. He helped Albion win both the League Cup (1966) and FA Cup (1968) and also played in the 1967 and 1970 League Cup finals. He was voted Midland Footballer of the Year on three occasions (1969, 1971 and 1979) and topped the First Division scoring charts in 1970/71 with 28 goals. It was Brown who netted the winning goal at Boundary Park that took Albion back into the First Division in 1976. The picture below shows Tony celebrating after scoring Albion's winning goal at Leicester in February 1972.

Albion defenders John Wile (5) and Ally Robertson (6) attempting (in vain) to stop Justin Fashanu (8) getting in a header for Norwich City during a League game at The Hawthorns in September 1980. The game ended in a 3-0 win for the Baggies in front of 15,414 spectators.

Cyrille Regis and Aston Villa's defender Allan Evans contest a high ball during the local derby at The Hawthorns in November 1980. In another League game on Albion soil in May 1982, Regis was sent-off for aiming a punch at the Villa star – and in 1999/2000 both men were together at The Hawthorns as part of manager Brian Little's coaching staff!

Albion were going through a difficult period in the mid-1980s and after a run of 10 defeats in 14 matches halfway through the 1983/84 season Johnny Giles was brought back for his second spell as manager. He didn't get off to the greatest of starts, Albion losing 1-0 to Third Division Plymouth Argyle in a fifth round FA Cup-tie at The Hawthorns. The former Irish international brought his brother-in-law Nobby Stiles, the ex-Manchester United and England World Cup star, and his former Leeds United colleague Norman Hunter as a back-up team. Unfortunately, things didn't work out second time round for Giles and he left in September 1985 after seventeen months in charge. The photograph shows Stiles, Giles and Hunter leaving the dug-out after Albion had lost to Plymouth.

Left: Striker Garry Thompson (seen here heading the ball) was signed by manager John Wiley from Coventry City for £225,000 in February 1983. It was hoped that 'Thommo' would link up with Cyrille Regis in the Baggies' attack. They did to a certain extent until October 1984 – when Regis was sold to Coventry! Thompson went on to score 45 goals in 105 games for Albion before joining Sheffield Wednesday for £450,000 in August 1985. *Right*: George 'Mother' Reilly, a tall, gangly striker, took over Thompson's jersey in December 1985, having been signed from Newcastle United for £200,000. He had done well with his previous clubs but never really made an impact with Albion and after scoring 10 goals in 50 first team outings he moved to Cambridge on a free transfer in June 1988.

Pictured here during a home League game against Reading, Don Goodman (left) waits for a slip as fellow striker Bobby Williamson, a Scot signed from Rangers in August 1986, is foiled by goalkeeper Steve Francis.

Left: Don Goodman moved to The Hawthorns from Bradford City for £50,000. Admired by the fans, over the next four years he scored 63 goals in 181 appearances for the Baggies before transferring to Sunderland (perhaps against his wishes) for £900,000. He later played for Wolves (where he teamed up with another ex-Albion star Steve Bull), Barnsley and Motherwell. *Right*: Kevin Bartlett was at The Hawthorns with Goodman. Although he was a striker with pace and good finishing power, he perhaps found the going too tough for him at Albion and after scoring 11 goals in 43 appearances he moved to Notts County.

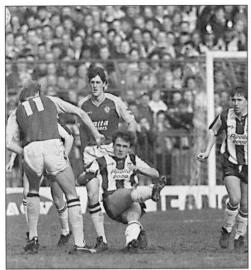

Left: Action from the fifth round FA Cup-tie between Albion and Aston Villa at The Hawthorns in February 1990. Bernard McNally (centre) and Gary Robson (right), who formed part of the Albion midfield during the early 1990s, face the two Ians, Ormondroyd (11) and Olney. Villa won the game 2-0. McNally, a Northern Ireland international signed from Shrewsbury Town for £385,000 in June 1989, remained at the club for six years during which time he scored 23 goals in 282 appearances and helped Albion win promotion in 1993. Robson, the younger brother of Bryan, played in 282 senior matches for Albion, scoring 35 goals. He could also occupy a striker's role and did well when leading the attack. He moved to Bradford City in 1993 shortly after his testimonial match against Aston Villa. *Right*: Romeo Zondervan made his debut in English football as a substitute for Albion against Middlesbrough at Ayresome Park on 9 March 1982. Less than four weeks later, with only six League games under his belt, he played in the FA Cup semi-final defeat by QPR at Highbury. A talented player able to occupy a variety of positions, Zondervan followed fellow Dutchman Maarten Jol to The Hawthorns from FC Twente Enschede when he was signed by Ronnie Allen for £225,000. Zondervan scored 5 goals in 95 appearances for Albion before moving to Ipswich Town in March 1984 for a cut-price fee of just £70,000. He played in over 300 senior matches for the Portman Road club.

In the summer of 1983 Albion signed a lucrative sponsorship deal with the local Sandwell Council. This picture shows members of the council with players Cyrille Regis (left) and Derek Statham (right) along with Baggies chairman Sid Lucas (next to Staham) at the press conference at The Hawthorns.

The former Ipswich, Arsenal, Watford and England international Brian Talbot was signed by Albion from Stoke for £25,000 in January 1988. At the time the Baggies were twentieth in the Second Division with relegation starring them in the face. Manager Ron Atkinson had chosen Talbot to boost the midfield and he became an instant hit with the fans, his influence and experience helping the team beat the drop. Halfway through the next season Talbot took over as player-manager and Albion looked promotion material until a disappointing sequence of results (three wins from the last ten games) saw them finish a disappointing ninth. However, after another poor campaign when they finished twentieth, performances got worse and in January 1991 after non-League Woking had humiliated Albion 4-2 in the FA Cup at The Hawthorns, Talbot lost his job having scored 6 goals in 83 games for the club. Bobby Gould replaced Talbot, but he failed miserably and at the end of the season, after drawing six of their last seven matches (all 1-1), Third Division football came to The Hawthorns for the first time in the club's history. Albion finally slipped through the trap door in the city of Bath on 11 May 1991 after failing to beat Bristol Rovers at Twerton Park.

Clive Whitehead (right) as Albion captain with his counterpart Joe Waters of Grimsby Town prior to a testimonial match at Blundell Park for the Mariners midfielder in 1984. Whitehead was signed from Bristol City for £100,000 in November 1981 and was able to play at full-back, as an orthodox left-winger or in midfield. An excellent footballer, he spent six years at The Hawthorns during which time he appeared in almost 200 first-class matches, scoring 9 goals. Whitehead also played for Wolves (on loan), Portsmouth and Exeter City before returning to Ashton Gate as a coach.

Ten
Disappointment and Renewal

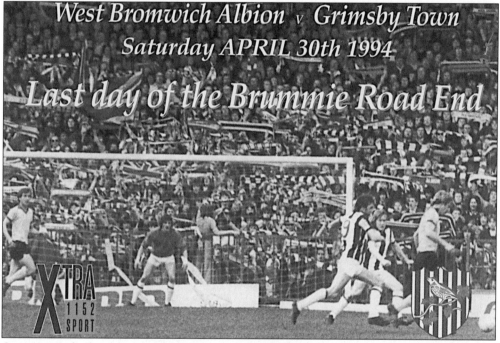

West Bromwich Albion v Grimsby Town
Saturday APRIL 30th 1994
Last day of the Brummie Road End

Over a period of eighteen years (1976 to 1994) practically the whole of The Hawthorns was redeveloped. Initially fourteen executive boxes were installed under the Rainbow Stand with an extra 750 paddock seats inserted in front of the boxes themselves. In 1977 the Executive Box complex was completed while the terracing at both the Smethwick and Birmingham Road Ends of the ground were made safer by the placement of extra crush-barriers. In 1979 work started on the new £2.5 million Halfords Lane Stand. This was built in two phases and catered for 4,500 spectators (all seated). Over thirty more executive boxes were installed and there were new facilities for the manager, coaching staff, players, the chairman and his fellow directors, VIPs visiting the club, the press, executive club members, office staff, shop personnel and a lot more. In 1985 a new roof was fitted over the Smethwick End. Soon afterwards a state-of-the-art crowd control video system was introduced and over a four-year period (1988 to 1992) more safety work was carried out at the ground with a new sponsor's lounge being opened on the Halfords Lane/Birmingham Road corner. The playing area was returfed in 1990 and in 1992 the roof over the Smethwick End terracing was removed as part of the redevelopment which would eventually result in an all-seater stadium. This was completed in 1994 at a cost of £4.15 million, of which Albion were to receive almost £2.1 million from the Football Trust.

The old players' lounge at The Hawthorns before the development of the stadium.

West Bromwich Albion Football Club

A view of The Hawthorns in 1992 just after the roof had been taken away from the Smethwick End. The newly modernised, all-seater Hawthorns stadium was officially opened on Boxing Day 1994 when Bristol City were beaten 1-0 in a Division One game in front of 21,071 spectators. The capacity of The Hawthorns in 2000 was 25,296. When the ground was opened in 1900 it could house 35,000 fans. The capacity rose to 70,000 by 1926 and since 1954 (the last time a 60,000 crowd assembled there for an cup-tie with Newcastle United) the capacity has slowly decreased. There are plans to increase the capacity of the ground to over 30,000 – and one sincerely hopes that when that takes effect Albion will be playing in the Premiership!

The 'old' Birmingham Road End, once capable of housing 14,000 spectators (all standing).

The 'new' Apollo 2000 Stand at the Birmingham Road End with its 8,286 seats.

In the summer of 1992, Argentinian World Cup star and former Tottenham Hotspur midfielder Ossie Ardiles was appointed manager at The Hawthorns, taking over from Gould. He brought with him (from White Hart Lane) Keith Burkinshaw, who was later to take over as Albion boss following Ardiles' departure after just one season in charge. But what a season it turned out to be, Albion gaining promotion at Wembley via the play-offs. The picture here shows Albion chairman Trevor Summers flanked by Burkinshaw (left) and Ardiles (right).

Nicky Reid, the former Manchester City player, scored only one goal for Albion – but what a crucial one – the second in the play-off final victory against Port Vale in 1993. Albion had began 1992/93 very well, winning seven and drawing one of their first nine League games. They didn't do too well in October or early November but an excellent run of results saw them beaten only once in the League between 21 November and the end of January. Three defeats were suffered in February but with the driving force of Ardiles behind them and the goals flowing from Bob Taylor, the best signing made by Bobby Gould, and Andy Hunt, secured initially on loan from Newcastle United, Albion stormed into the play-offs. They met and defeated Swansea City over two legs before playing Port Vale at Wembley for a place in the Division One. Over 42,000 fans followed the Baggies to the Empire Stadium where they celebrated in style, boing-boinging all the way home after a brilliant 3-0 victory. Unfortunately, during the summer Ardiles was lured away by Spurs as Albion set about consolidating themselves in a higher division.

A ticket for that 1993 encounter at Wembley.

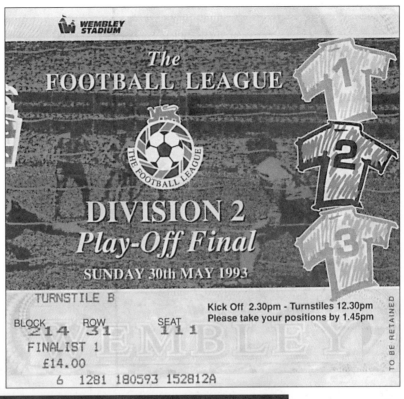

WEMBLEY STADIUM

The
FOOTBALL LEAGUE

DIVISION 2
Play-Off Final
SUNDAY 30th MAY 1993

TURNSTILE B

Kick Off 2.30pm - Turnstiles 12.30pm
Please take your positions by 1.45pm

BLOCK	ROW	SEAT
214	31	111

FINALIST 1
£14.00
6   1281   180593   152812A

TO BE RETAINED

Andy Hunt became only the tenth Albion player to score at Wembley when he put the Baggies ahead in the 1993 play-off final. Hunt went on to net 85 goals for Albion in 240 outings before joining Charlton Athletic as they entered the Premiership.

Hundreds of Baggies supporters admired the determination and commitment of central defender Gary Strodder, pictured here challenging former Albion and Northern Ireland forward Robbie Dennison during a local derby with Wolves at The Hawthorns. He was a terrific competitor, always giving 110 per cent out on the field, never shirking a tackle and a battler to the end. He joined Albion from West Ham for £190,000 in August 1990 and made 166 appearances for the club (9 goals scored) before moving to Notts County for £145,000 in July 1995. He played superbly well in the 1993 play-off final at Wembley alongside Paul Raven.

Steve Lilwall (on the extreme right of the picture), preparing to challenge former Albion star Kevin Kent at snow-covered Vale Park, had a tremendous first season in League football. Signed from Kidderminster Harriers to replace Graham Harbey at left-back, he made 44 out of a possible 46 League appearances in 1992/93 and then played his part in Albion's victory over Port Vale in the play-off final.

Above left: Stuart Naylor, punching clear during the Oldham *v*. Albion League game at Boundary Park, made more senior appearances than any other Albion goalkeeper, amassing 410 between February 1986 and August 1996. Signed for £110,000 from Lincoln City, Naylor was beaten by two Jesper Olsen penalties on his Baggies' debut at Old Trafford when Manchester United won 3-0, but he became a very consistent performer and thoroughly deserved his testimonial before leaving for Bristol City. *Above right*: Dave Gilbert (8) was an Alan Buckley signing from Grimsby Town in August 1995. A 5ft 4in left-sided midfielder, he had previously served with Lincoln, Scunthorpe and Northampton and when he arrived at Albion he had already made more than 200 first-class appearances. He had 76 outings for the Baggies before leaving in 1998. *Right*: Kevin Donovan played for Huddersfield Town and Halifax before joining Albion for £70,000 in October 1992. A talented right-sided midfielder, he was fast and clever, netting 32 goals in 203 appearances before leaving to join his former boss Alan Buckley at Grimsby for £300,000 in July 1997. Donovan scored Albion's third goal in the 1993 play-off final.

Above left: Former Ajax and Fortuna Sittard midfielder Richard Sneekes was signed from Bolton Wanderers in March 1996 for £385,000. He scored 10 goals in his first 13 League outings for Albion to save the Baggies from relegation. During the year 2000 the long-haired Sneekes passed the milestone of 250 senior appearances in English football – and again helped Albion stay in the First Division. *Above right*: Raven-haired central defender Shaun Murphy made his Football League debut for Notts County before joining Albion for £500,000 in December 1996. He remained at The Hawthorns until May 1999 when he moved to Sheffield United having amassed 78 appearances for the Baggies (7 goals scored). He is now an Australian international, having earlier been in his country's Olympic Games squad. *Left*: Daryl Burgess celebrated thirteen years' service with Albion in July 2000 (eleven as a professional). In that time the Birmingham-born defender accumulated 372 senior appearances (13 goals) and played with a dozen different partners in the centre of Albion's back-line, always giving a solid and determined performance.

Having first played in the Anglo-Italian Cup competition in 1970, Albion were involved in the same tournament again during the mid-1990s and they came mighty close to making it to the Wembley final in 1996. Having drawn 0-0 in Salernitana, lost 2-1 at home to Foggia, beat Reggiana (h) 2-1, defeated Brescia 1-0 on a snow-covered pitch in Italy and ousted rivals Birmingham City 4-1 on penalties (after a 2-2 draw at St Andrew's), Albion played their old adversaries Port Vale in the English 'final' but were beaten over two legs (drawing 0-0 at home and losing 3-1 in the Potteries). These two pictures show Albion lining up before the game in Brescia – which was attended by just 196 supporters! The team photograph (below) shows, from left to right, back row: Ian Hamilton, Stuart Naylor, Daryl Burgess, Bob Taylor, Paul Raven. Front row: Paul Edwards, Kevin Donovan, David Smith, Dave Gilbert, Julian Darby, Tony Rees. Bob Taylor scored the winning goal three minutes from time.

Sean Flynn, a hard-working, courageous midfielder played over 100 times for Coventry City, had 65 outings for Derby County and 5 on loan with Stoke City before joining Albion for £260,000 in August 1997. He became skipper at The Hawthorns and made over 120 appearances for the Baggies. A workaholic, Flynn supported Albion as a youngster, watching his heroes from the Birmingham Road terracing. He was released in May 2000 by new manager Gary Megson a week after Albion had retained their First Division status and has now joined Tranmere Rovers.

Kevin 'Killer' Kilbane – a big favourite with the Albion supporters – was a club record signing at £1 million from Preston North End in June 1997. A Republic of Ireland international with tremendous pace, excellent ball skills and powerful shot, he scored 18 goals in 122 appearances for Albion before moving to Premiership side Sunderland for £2.5 million in December 1999 – to the obvious disappointment of the diehard fans. The picture here shows Kilbane driving towards goal during Albion's home League game with Norwich City on the opening day of the 1999/2000 season.

Prior to the start of the 1996/97 season, Albion played in and won the International Football Festival competition on the Isle of Wight. Bury, Isle of Man, Port Vale, previous winners Wigan Athletic and the holders Wrexham also took part in the annual event. Albion won their three games – 1-0 *v.* Wigan (Paul Groves the scorer), 2-0 *v.* Port Vale (Andy Hunt and Bob Taylor on target) and then 1-0 *v.* Bury in the final, Taylor again the marksman. *Top left*: The cover of the tournament programme. *Top right*: A delighted Bob Taylor holds aloft the festival trophy. *Below*: The team photograph taken before the final against Bury. From left to right (players only), back row: Shane Nicholson, Nigel Spink, Shaun Cunnington, Andy Hunt, Daryl Burgess, Paul Groves. Front row: Bob Taylor (with mascot), Richard Sneekes, Paul Holmes, Julian Darby, Paul Raven. Gary Germaine, Kevin Donovan and Paul Perschisolido were second-half substitutes.

127

Signed from Calgiari, Italian midfielder Enzo Maresca was a big hit with the Albion supporters before being sold to Juventus for a club record £4.3 million in January 2000.

Left: Bob Taylor returned to The Hawthorns for a second spell in March 2000 – re-signed from Bolton Wanderers – and duly helped Albion stave off relegation. *Right:* Hot shot Lee Hughes, a £250,000 signing from Kidderminster Harriers in 1997, has already written himself into the club's record books. Hopefully, there are a lot more goals to come.